"As a huge fan of healthy and easy, my copy of this book will be dog-eared in no time! The majority of these recipes have five ingredients or fewer (see, I can do this!), and they all have my #1 recipe requirement—the real stuff—nothing fake or processed. Back to basics is best, and *The Best Homemade Kids' Snacks on the Planet* is jam-packed with the best snack ideas for your kids!"

—Kelly Lester, founder of easylunchboxes.com

"I have trouble getting my three year old to eat real meals so I love having this seemingly endless source of healthy snack ideas. He doesn't need to know that his Super Green Smoothie or Chocolate Avocado Pudding is actually nutritious ... shhhh!"

—Heather Gibbs Flett, co-author of *The Rookie Mom's Handbook* and co-founder of rookiemoms.com

THE BEST HOMEMADE KIDS' SNACKS ON THE PLANET

More than 200 Healthy Homemade Snacks You and Your Kids Will Love

Laura Fuentes
Founder of MOMables.com

Fair Winds Press
100 Cummings Center, Suite 406L
Beverly, MA 01915

fairwindspress.com • quarryspoon.com

First published in the USA in 2015 by
Fair Winds Press, a member of
Quarto Publishing Group USA Inc.
100 Cummings Center
Suite 406-L
Beverly, MA 01915-6101
www.fairwindspress.com
Visit www.QuarrySPOON.com and help us celebrate food and culture one spoonful at a time!

19 18 17 16 15 1 2 3 4 5

ISBN: 978-1-59233-661-6

Digital edition published in 2015
eISBN: 978-1-62788-281-1

Library of Congress Cataloging-in-Publication Data

Fuentes, Laura (Chef)
  The best homemade kids' snacks on the planet : more than 200
healthy homemade snacks you and your kids will love / Laura Fuentes,
founder of MOMables.com.
    pages cm
  ISBN 978-1-59233-663-0 -- ISBN 978-1-62788-281-1 (eISBN)
  1. Snack foods. I. Title.
  TX740.F767 2015
  641.5'3--dc23
                                                        2014047820

Cover design: Carol Holtz

Page layout: *tabula rasa* graphic design
Photography: Alison Bickel Photography (www.alisonbickel.com)

Printed and bound in China

The information in this book is for educational purposes only. It is not intended to replace the advice of a physician or medical practitioner. Please see your health care provider before beginning any new health program.

For my kids, Sofia, Alex, and Gabriel. You make my world a better place.

CONTENTS

INTRODUCTION

"Mom, can we have a snack?" Do you hear this question all the time at your house? I do! When our days are packed with activities, homemade snacks are a great way for my kids and their friends to fill their bellies with good, fresh food between meals.

I grew up in Spain where fruit was the only snack option. In fact, the whole concept of "snacking" was quite foreign to me until I moved to the United States and had kids of my own. Of course, things are a bit different now. As a mom, I'm constantly on the move with my three kids, working our way through a busy schedule filled with after-school activities, play dates, classroom parties, sports, birthday parties, and lots of other social gatherings. With so much time spent outside the home, on-the-go food logistics can become an issue. We also have to accommodate everything from allergies to personal taste preferences, and no one wants to do that with a prepackaged, not-so-healthy choice, right?

As the founder of MOMables.com, I'm also always working on recipes for the MOMables community and remaking prepackaged foods into homemade versions. Our lifestyle is busy and hectic and, like most parents, I use convenient snacks to help me out often. As a mom running a company with the sole purpose of helping parents make fresh foods appealing to kids, you could say I've become snack obsessed!

Of course, my kids have fully embraced the art of snacking, so utilizing fresh real ingredients in my recipes is very important. I'm not sure if it's because I'm always testing recipes for them or because I am constantly receiving samples of single-serve items conveniently sold as snacks, but at times it seems as if we are all snacking. A lot!

I will tell you this, though: Going to the grocery store with three kids in tow isn't fun. It's as if the brightly colored boxes are calling their names and all of a sudden, they are starving! On more than one embarrassing occasion (I'm sure you've probably had one too!), I've had to open cheese sticks for everyone, allowed my youngest to eat a banana, even opened a bag of nuts in the middle of the store! Why do those snack boxes have to be so colorful and appealing to kids? Ah, yes … marketing.

But a trip down the snack aisles at the grocery store can be more than a little discouraging. Boxed goodies piled from floor to ceiling are just waiting to be purchased and gobbled up by young and old alike. Buying snacks nowadays can be a complicated endeavor.

Designed to be convenient, portable, and tasty, most boxed snacks come with big promises and little nutritional value.

I used to take comfort in buying whole grain, naturally sweetened, healthy-labeled snacks for my kids. I believed that those with the organic label had better ingredients, were less processed, and were healthier than the conventional ones. But during my journey as a parent and snack expert, I've learned that kids need to snack on real foods, ideally, snacks that are minimally processed, contain no unidentifiable ingredients, and better yet, have been made at home.

On occasion, I find myself buying boxed snacks because I haven't figured out how to re-create my kids' favorites at home. Coincidentally, in 2014, I competed (and won!) in a Food Network television show called *Rewrapped*, where I had to re-create a popular snack food. Ultimately, there is no challenge I won't take on, and many of the recipes in this book are no different. Even the most unhealthy snack foods from the store can be replicated in a healthier, wholesome way at home—and it's easier than you think!

In this book you'll find lots of recipes that make fruit and veggies more appealing, easy ways to dress up basic ingredients, and homemade versions of classic store-bought snacks. Some recipes are clearly intended as treats, so I'll leave portioning to your discretion.

As a full-time working mom of young kids, I, like you, struggle to find the time to get it all done. It's because of this and my family's love for snacks that this book has become a reality. I know you're busy, and you want the best for your kids. Inside you'll find many of my time-saving and prep-ahead tips, storage ideas, ingredient substitutions, allergy-friendly options, and transportation how-tos—basically every secret in my snack-making arsenal!

From this day forward, together, we can feed our kids uncomplicated, freshly made foods using real ingredients that are much more nutritious than the store-bought alternatives. Start here and you'll pave a path of health and wellness for your children starting with the snacks and treats they love.

A final note before we dive in; the recipes in this book come with the support of an active community of thousands of parents who, with my help, are feeding their kids real food they love over at MOMables.com. If and when you're ready, join us!

Now, let's get snackin'!

CHAPTER 1

FOR THE LOVE
OF SNACKS

Do your kids love to snack more than they like
to eat their meals? If so, you are not alone. With
the recipes in this book, you'll never run out of
awesome snack ideas. Expensive, processed
boxed snacks? Those will be a thing of the past!

Store-Bought vs. Homemade

For a few years after my oldest came of snacking age, I bought packaged snacks from the store. Most were labeled "whole grain" and "organic" and claimed to be nutritious.

But in reality, what we trade for the "ease" of buying prepackaged snacks is nutrition and our children's health. Many of the ingredients—including artificial sweeteners, preservatives, emulsifiers, stabilizers, coloring dyes, and leavening agents—have been linked to health risks, autoimmune diseases, and even cancer. I don't know about you, but I've had enough!

And what about cost? The ingredients in boxed snacks can come at a cost to your family's health while also making a dent in your wallet. When I removed the packaged snacks and convenience items from my grocery list, my food budget stretched tremendously. I had more money available to buy better ingredients to make all of our favorite foods. Simply put, it is much cheaper to make your own snacks than it is to buy ready-made ones.

Health risks and food budget have played the biggest role in my decision to make my own snacks from scratch. You can make many of the same treats that your kids already love with real ingredients! I'm not a low fat, zero sugar, low carb kind of gal, though, so you won't find any recipes of that kind on these pages. But I am a *real-ingredient* and *everything-in-moderation* kind of person. I like our snacks to be healthful, varied, and delicious, unlike their store-bought counterparts, which tend to lack both nutrition and flavor.

What's more, I don't feel like I'm depriving my kids of anything by making homemade snacks. I know my kids will get plenty of these packaged items when they are in other environments, like at someone else's home or away at day camp. For this reason, I do my best to make sure they eat the best ingredients possible when they are at home, at school eating their lunches, and while we're out enjoying activities with the snacks we bring with us. Simply put, the benefits of making your own snacks at home far outweigh the time and elbow grease you'll put into making them.

Finally, get your kids involved, especially the older ones! Use their favorite recipes to teach them kitchen skills, as well as the responsibility of meal and snack preparation and kitchen cleanup. Make it fun for all of you!

The Homemade Snacks Pantry

When you think of making homemade snacks in your own kitchen, does your mind immediately race to all the ingredients that you would need to keep on hand in your pantry and fridge? Or perhaps your heart skips a few beats because you can't help but translate all those ingredients into the additional money required to buy them? If so, I completely understand.

But realize that the long-term cost of stocking your pantry for homemade recipes will in fact be cheaper than buying premade, packaged snacks at the store. Nearly all the recipes in this book have very basic ingredients that can be found at your local grocery store and, while you might have to purchase a few items, the price per snack works out to be incredibly reasonable and frugal.

Making snacks quickly and easily is simple when you stock your pantry well. Here is how I keep my pantry stocked so I can make homemade foods at any time.

HAVE A PLAN FOR YOUR SNACKS

If you're already a meal planner, you know how much time this practice can save you in the long run. But even if you're not keen to plan every meal for every day, I encourage you to at least select a few snacks at the start of your week and add the required ingredients to your shopping list. That way, you can buy—and maybe even prep—for the week all at once, and skip buying the boxed versions. Having a plan can save you money by reducing ingredient waste, reduce stress, and help you feel more prepared for the week ahead.

MAKE A LIST

I keep a notepad stuck to the side of my pantry where I write the ingredients I'll need to replenish on my next trip to the grocery store. Keeping an up-to-date list of these items allows me to save money by avoiding impulse purchases or buying something we don't actually need just because I'm not sure if we're running low.

BUY IN BULK

When buying ingredients for baked goods (usually kid favorites), keep in mind that it is significantly cheaper to buy in bulk. Items such as grains and nuts are much cheaper when purchased in larger quantities, and, while it will cost a tad more up front, if you spread out the cost over multiple recipes and multiple snacks, your dollar actually stretches much further than it would if you were buying those same ingredients in smaller quantities and replenishing more frequently.

Many bulk items also keep very well when stored properly. Keep flours and nuts in a cool, dry, dark place—or in your freezer for even longer shelf life.

Pantry Necessities

Flours, Grains, and Seeds
Whole-wheat flour
All-purpose flour
Oats and oat flour*
Coconut flour or other flours for specialty diets
Grains of your choice (such as quinoa or rice, etc.)
Corn kernels for popping
Flaxseed or flax meal
Chia seeds

Baking Supplies and Sweeteners

Honey
Pure maple syrup
Sugar
Coconut oil
Baking soda
Baking powder
Salt
Pure vanilla extract and/or vanilla beans
Dried fruits
Nuts
Chocolate chips
Cocoa powder

Refrigerated Items

Butter
Milk
Eggs
Cheese
Yogurt

Other

Nut butters (or nut-free alternatives)
Coconut milk (canned)
Bananas
Fresh fruit and vegetables

*To make oat flour at home, simply place oats in a food processor or blender and grind until it has a flourlike texture.

Making Snacks Portable

Half the battle with making all the snacks your children want and need is knowing how to package and transport them to activities and outings. I often have the greatest recipe ideas and execute them flawlessly, but when it comes time to pack it in my bag to take in the car, things fall apart—literally.

Thankfully, this book steers you clear of that. Most of the recipes here can be transported on large trays, in individual bags or cups, or in leak-proof containers. You know those cupcake carrying trays? I use those to transport a lot more than just cupcakes! I love how they cover but don't smoosh the foods, so I often place my cookies and other delicate snacks inside. Airtight containers also help keep your fresh-baked snacks fresher for a longer period of time. Less air passing through your container means you won't have issues with crackers and other goodies getting stale.

For smaller portions, bento-style lunch boxes can do double duty as snack containers. These containers have separate sections to keep hot/cold and wet/dry items from mixing and creating gross concoctions. The compartments are great for holding dips, veggies, fruit, chips and other dip-friendly items.

Thermoses are also your absolute best friends. A stainless steel, double-insulated thermos should be in everyone's tool kit! They are perfect for keeping frozen snacks cold and hot snacks toasty, even on the go.

Your thermos is also a fantastic way to transport smoothies. Smoothies are easy and fast to make on a hectic morning and they are a great way to work fruits, vegetables, and yogurt into one nutrient-packed, satisfying snack. Best of all, smoothies are the perfect afternoon pick-me-up when you're rushing hungry kids out the door to outdoor activities. Simply hand them a smoothie in a leak proof container and you are good to go!

Laura's Tip

To prechill your thermos, store it inside your freezer for at least 1 hour.

A leak-proof container is key! Kids drop things and don't always place cups perfectly in cup holders ... imagine a leaky container on its side in the backseat. Trust me; it's no fun to clean up day-old, dried-up smoothie on the seats of your car! To avoid this, look for an insulated thermos with a straw and a secure lid, and, when filling any container, be sure to leave a little room for movement during transport—about ¼ inch (6 mm).

Many of the recipes in this book include a Kitchen Note or Laura's Tip, both of which provide suggestions for the proper way to store and transport recipes for on-the-go snacking. By following these tips, not only will your snacks be homemade and delicious, they will be long-lasting too!

Laura's Tip

Kids love thermoses and water bottles with straws, but they can get dirty very quickly and wear out fast. Here are some ways to keep containers and straws safely sanitized and free of debris so that they're clean and last as long as possible:

- Keep a baby bottle brush on hand near the sink. They are the perfect size for getting down into drink containers.
- Mix equal parts vinegar and water and let straws soak regularly. This formula works as a natural cleaning and sanitizing agent. After soaking, wash normally and let dry.
- Stick them in the dishwasher! Most straws are sturdy enough to be washed with the other dishes, but check manufacturer specifications to be sure.
- Use a pipe cleaner or straw brush to thoroughly clean inside a straw.

Mastering the Snack Kitchen: Preparation, Freezing, and Storage Tips

Whipping up homemade snacks in a matter of minutes can be nearly impossible when you are knee-deep in breakfast, lunch, or dinner preparation. Remember that a little planning goes a long way. If your oven is on from roasting vegetables for dinner, why not make some muffins, cookies, or a loaf of bread while the oven is hot and your kitchen already looks as if a tornado swept through it?

Do plan on making multiple snacks at once, which saves tons of time later on. You can even coordinate recipes so that ingredients overlap, saving both time and money. I guarantee that a bit of prep ahead of time can be life changing!

When it comes to making dinner and lunch, I live by the saying, "Cook once, eat (at least) twice." Why should it be any different when it comes to making snacks? It shouldn't! Say you are making homemade banana chips for this afternoon's snack. Don't just make enough for today, double or triple the recipe and store what doesn't get eaten for another day of the week or even next week. Do this with a few snacks each time and you can keep a variety of snacks in rotation while maintaining a stocked pantry.

Aside from my big-batch advice, here are a few additional tips for feeding your family real food snacks while still managing to keep up with your busy life.

PREP-AHEAD AND FREEZING

Did you know that muffin and cupcake batters can be frozen in their individual paper cups? Simply place the liners in the baking pan, fill with batter, and transfer the pan to the freezer for a few hours. Once frozen, remove the individual cups from the pan and transfer to a zip-top freezer bag. Remember to label the bag with cooking time and temperature.

When you have a freezer full of several different muffins, snack time can be as easy as preheating the oven and baking them!

To prepare your frozen raw batter, remove the desired number of cupcakes or muffins from the freezer, place inside a muffin tin, and let them thaw to room temperature while the oven preheats. Then, bake as usual! This strategy allows you to bake fresh treats whenever you want or need them. Plus, frozen foods last quite a bit longer than foods stored in the refrigerator or at room temperature, so there's no need to fret about them getting moldy in the fridge if you've made too many.

Speaking of eating things before they get moldy, be sure to wash and chop all fruits and vegetables as soon as you get them home. Don't wait till you need them! When fruit is washed and ready to eat, you're more likely to use it in recipes and your family is more likely to eat it before it goes bad.

Did you know that strawberries and blueberries last longer if you simply wash them properly? I use 1 cup (240 ml) white vinegar, 1 small pump of dish soap, and 4 cups (946 ml) water to make a bath for the berries. This process washes away dirt and kills most of the mold spores and bacteria present on the fruit. After soaking, rinse and dry the berries well and store in an airtight container in the refrigerator.

Laura's Tip

Learn how to make berries last longer in this video: http://bit.ly/berriesthatlast.

Dietary Restrictions and Substitutions

In early 2013, while writing *The Best Homemade Kids' Lunches on the Planet* (Fair Winds Press, 2014), I had to make drastic dietary changes in my own family's diet. We were all experiencing significant health issues that were only going to be remedied by making some real changes in what we were eating. We were eating healthy already, thank goodness, but more changes needed to be made.

Luckily for my family, I know how to adapt recipes to fit our needs. There are also thousands of parents in the MOMables community who feel challenged by their own family's dietary restrictions. When I sat down to develop recipes for this book, I really wanted to create a guide for homemade snacking. Most of the recipes in this book include fresh fruit and many are centered around how to get our kids to eat more veggies.

I feel that when we prioritize the fruits and veggies as our primary source for nourishment in between meals, we can keep food allergy concerns to a minimum. Fortunately, there are many fantastic substitutes available at the store for items that traditionally contain gluten. For example, the Chocolate Banana Mini Pretzel-wiches (page 67) were photographed with gluten free mini pretzels, since that's all we have in our house.

My oldest son eats a gluten free diet, my youngest son eats dairy free, and I eliminated all grain from my own diet. Needless to say, making meals and snacks can be a little more challenging these days, and I've gone through periods during which I definitely felt like a short-order cook.

Because I know many of your families have dietary restrictions and require recipe modifications, I've done my best to cover substitutions throughout the book. There are few recipes that contain non-negotiable substitutions, but for the most part, I've done my best to create recipes that are already free of refined sugars, easily adaptable with an all-purpose gluten free flour mix, have the ability to become dairy free by using nondairy milk and can be nut free when you use a nut butter alternative.

Just as in *The Best Homemade Kids' Lunches on the Planet*, in this book I focus on whole, real-food ingredients, and simple-to-make recipes. Because the meals and snacks I create are based on those principles, substitutions for common allergens are simple to make and you'll find suggestions throughout.

If you modify a recipe successfully, don't be afraid to make a note right on the page or in the Feedback Charts, pages 222—232. My favorite cookbooks are filled with sticky notes containing recipe modifications that fit my family.

Of course, if you are making snacks for your child's classroom, it's important to ask the teacher if any of the children suffer from known food allergies, nuts being the most critical. For this reason alone, I always suggest using a nut-free alternative or selecting a recipe that is completely nut free. The good news is that in this book you have more than 200 recipes to choose from!

My hope is that you are able to expand your allergy-friendly recipe repertoire and ditch some of your go-to store-bought snacks. I believe the recipes in this book are simple enough for anyone to make, with ingredients easily available at your local grocery store or online. And trust me, since I've got my own dietary restrictions in my household, I've tested lots of substitutions and have found these homemade snacks are just as delicious as their allergen-filled counterparts.

Snacking Rules

In the process of testing recipes for this book, I would ask my friends to come over with their kids to sample some of the goodies. One day, my friend Jessica wanted to know how she could introduce new foods to her picky eaters at mealtime because her kids never seemed to want to eat anything. She described them as being "super picky."

Surely, no kid would refuse her delicious homemade meals (I've tried them), so I asked her about their snacking habits.

Me: *Do your kids like snacks?*
Jessica: *My kids LOVE snacks!*
Me: *Do they ask for snacks often?*
Jessica: *That's all they ask for!*
Me: *Do you have snacking rules at your house?*
Jessica: *Rules? What rules? There are snacking rules?*

As I mentioned earlier, the whole snacking concept was pretty new to me until I had kids. My grandmother's definition of a snack was synonymous with fruit, so the fact that there are more than 200 recipes in this book and many include fresh fruit shows you how much influence our upbringing can have on our choices.

When my kids ask for snack, my first question is, "What kind of fruit would you like?" Sometimes, that discourages them from eating any snack because they argue that they just had fruit earlier.

For me, it's important to find out if my child is hungry, bored, or thirsty. Sometimes, especially in the summer, my kids are dehydrated and yet they ask for snack. I also evaluate if they are actually eating their food at mealtime, and if not, I try to figure out why.

Am I giving them snack foods every few hours to entertain them, or are they snacking instead of drinking water, which is essential for their bodies to function? These are the types of questions I ask myself every time my kids request a snack. Sometimes, their growing bodies are just "hungry" and mealtime is at least three hours away.

The final "rule" that I follow at my house is called "snack cut-off time." My kids get home from school at 3:15 p.m. and 3:45 p.m. is my cut-off time for snacks, since dinner is served between 6:45 p.m. and 7:00 p.m. Allowing their bodies

enough time to develop an appetite is crucial to mealtime success; I don't want to jeopardize dinner by serving them a snack any later than the established cut-off time. As you know, kids will be kids and they'll ask for a snack again right before bed, but use your best judgment then (or go back to the fruit-only rule).

Let's Get Started!

If you want to learn how to make snacks from scratch, this book will give you a lot of opportunities. And, if you want to replace a store-bought favorite snack or treat with the homemade version, I've included an entire chapter filled with options!

Learning how to make new recipes can be a little bit challenging at first, so I always suggest mastering one recipe, one technique at a time. I've done my very best to re-create recipes in the simplest language, so even a kitchen novice (or an eager teenager) can follow and yield a successful recipe.

Many of the recipes in this book provide the perfect opportunity to teach your children how to measure ingredients, knead, whisk, sift, roll out dough, and my son's favorite: use the cookie scooper! By trying new recipes, getting your kids involved, and learning how to make new foods from scratch we are able to feed our families better, more nutritious food!

CHAPTER 2

FRUIT AND VEGGIE SNACKS

I, too, struggle to get my kids to eat more
fresh produce—mostly because they complain
that it's boring. With the recipes in this section,
you'll find your kids are having a lot more fun
as you incorporate more variety! And more
variety means more vitamins, antioxidants,
and fiber, along with the necessary fun, of course.

Apple Sandwiches

This recipe takes the classic snack of apples dipped in peanut butter for a spin. The granola adds an irresistible crunch kids often love!

2 apples, washed

¼ cup (65 g) almond butter

¼ cup (34 g) store-bought or homemade granola (page 131)

¼ cup (20 g) shredded coconut

Cut each apple into 4 horizontal slices, creating round, flat circles (with a hole in the center, like an O). Discard seeds and any pulp around the core.

Lay 4 apple circles on a plate. Spread almond butter on top of each slice, sprinkle with granola and shredded coconut, and top each sandwich with remaining apple slices. Serve immediately.

YIELD: 4 servings

Chocolate Avocado Pudding

This nutritious pudding is my answer to buying a few too many avocados on sale at the store! The sweet flavor of the bananas and the creaminess of the avocados make for a delicious, dessertlike snack.

2 avocados, peeled and pitted

3 very ripe bananas, peeled

3 tablespoons (60 g) honey

1 teaspoon vanilla extract

6 tablespoons (30 g) unsweetened cocoa powder

Place avocados, bananas, and honey into the bowl of a food processor or blender. Blend until smooth.

Add vanilla extract and unsweetened cocoa powder to avocado mixture and continue blending until thoroughly combined.

Divide pudding into 4 single-serve cups and refrigerate for at least 2 hours prior to serving. These are best served very cold.

YIELD: 4 servings

Baked Apple Pie Parfait

Not wanting to make apple pies from scratch, I settled for these baked apple pie parfaits instead. They are a lot easier to make and just as satisfying as the real thing.

1 apple, diced

2 teaspoons maple syrup

2 tablespoons (10 g) oats

1 teaspoon coconut oil, melted (plus more for greasing ramekins)

¼ teaspoon cinnamon

½ cup (115 g) vanilla yogurt

Position oven rack in the middle of the oven, and preheat the oven to 400°F (200°C) and grease ramekins with coconut oil.

In a small bowl, combine diced apples, maple syrup, oats, coconut oil, and cinnamon. Divide mixture into two individual baking ramekins.

Place the ramekins on a baking sheet and bake for 20 minutes. Remove from oven and allow it to cool to room temperature.

Top each ramekin with a dollop of yogurt and serve.

YIELD: 2 servings

Strawberry Applesauce

In the fall and winter when apples are plentiful, I use up the last of my frozen summer strawberries in this recipe. Of course, it has now become a year-round favorite, so in the summer, I use fresh berries.

8 cups (1 kg) apples, peeled and cored

4 cups (580 g) strawberries

½ cup (120 ml) water

⅓ cup (115 g) honey

1 teaspoon cinnamon

Coarsely chop apples and strawberries and transfer them into a large saucepan.

Add water, honey, and cinnamon to the fruit and bring to a boil. Reduce heat to a simmer and continue cooking, stirring occasionally, for 10 to 15 minutes, until the apples have softened.

Once apples are soft and berries have dissolved, remove from heat and allow the mixture to cool to room temperature.

Carefully transfer the mixture to a standard blender or use an immersion blender to blend fruit to desired consistency. If the sauce is too thick for your taste, add a little bit more water, ¼ cup (60 ml) at a time.

Divide into small glass jars and refrigerate.

YIELD: 12 servings

Aloha Cups

I love warm, sweet pineapple. It's the perfect topping for yogurt or ice cream! For a lighter treat that is just as delicious, serve the warm pineapple on its own.

3 cups (495 g) fresh pineapple chunks

2 teaspoons coconut oil

2 tablespoons (40 g) honey (optional)

Shredded coconut

Place coconut oil in a pan over medium low heat. Add pineapple and sauté for about 3 minutes, or until pineapple begins to release its juices.

Remove from heat and divide into 4 bowls. Drizzle with honey, and sprinkle with coconut.

YIELD: 4 servings

Tropical Parfait

In my dream vacation, I'd be eating this for breakfast and snack every day. This parfait has a little sweet and a little crunch in every bite.

½ cup (90 g) mango, diced

⅓ cup (77 g) plain yogurt

2 tablespoons (25 g) Tropical Snowman Trail Mix (page 130)

In a parfait dish or canning jar, layer mango and yogurt. Chill for 30 minutes.

Sprinkle trail mix over the top and serve.

YIELD: 1 serving

Grape and Granola Yogurt Parfait

This healthy twist on the standard granola yogurt parfait combines refreshing green and red grapes. Top with your favorite granola and add a lot of crunchy fun to your snack routine.

¾ cup (263 g) green grapes

¾ cup (263 g) red grapes

¾ cup (180 g) vanilla yogurt

¼ cup (50 g) Pantry Granola (page 131)

In a medium bowl, combine grapes and yogurt.

Spoon into two serving bowls, sprinkle with granola, and serve.

YIELD: 2 servings

Red, White, and Blue Parfait ▶

I'm a huge fan of berries. Not only do strawberries and blueberries contain antioxidants, vitamin C, and fiber, they look pretty together. When presented in this parfait, I am sure your kids will love them too.

¼ cup (64 g) strawberries, diced

⅓ cup (77 g) yogurt

¼ cup (38 g) blueberries

1 tablespoon (15 g) Pantry Granola (page 131)

Layer strawberries, yogurt, and blueberries inside a parfait glass or canning jar.

Sprinkle granola on top and serve.

YIELD: 1 serving

White Chocolate Raspberries

My youngest son can eat a pint of raspberries in a single sitting he loves them so much! Once in a while, I sneak a few white chocolate chips into the raspberries in his lunch as a treat. When he's done he exclaims, "Moooooorrrrree berrrryyyy chippps!" in his cutest, most irresistible toddler voice.

1 pint (290 g) raspberries, washed

⅓ cup (58 g) white chocolate chips

Wash the raspberries and lay them on a paper towel to soak up the excess water.

Gently place a white chocolate chip into the center of each raspberry. Serve immediately and enjoy.

YIELD: 2 to 3 servings

Chocolate Toffee Berries

I once tried one of these berries from a berry delivery service, and they were delicious. Not wanting to pay the steep price tag for their premium berries, I set out to make my own. They make a beautiful gift or an addition to a party platter.

¾ cup (131 g) chocolate chips

½ teaspoon coconut oil

24 strawberries

½ cup (88 g) toffee bits

In a double boiler, melt chocolate chips and coconut oil.

Dip berries in chocolate, about three-quarters of the way to the stem; place them on a parchment-lined baking sheet and sprinkle with toffee bits.

Chill until set, about 20 minutes.

YIELD: 24 servings

◀ Heavenly Bowl

Remember I told you how much I love berries? This recipe is an extension of that love. Surely, all things are better with homemade whipped cream.

2 cups (290 g) berries, such as blueberries and strawberries mixed

1 cup (235 ml) heavy whipping cream

2 tablespoons (30 g) sugar

Divide berries into 4 dessert dishes.

FOR THE WHIPPED CREAM: Pour whipping cream into a metal bowl and add the sugar. Whisk or beat with an electric mixer until the cream reaches stiff peaks.

Top berries with whipped cream and fold a few times. Alternatively, you can layer the berries and whipped cream.

Reserve any unused whipped cream, and store in an airtight container for up to 10 hours. When ready to use, whisk for 15 seconds.

YIELD: 4 servings

Easy Strawberry Cheesecake Bites

I can think of very few things better than cheesecake and strawberries. I especially love making these over the summer, when strawberries are abundant, ripe, and naturally sweet.

8 ounces (225 g) whipped cream cheese, at room temperature

½ cup (60 g) powdered sugar

3 tablespoons (21 g) graham cracker crumbs

16 medium to large strawberries, washed and hulled

In a food processor or with a hand mixer, combine cream cheese and powdered sugar and transfer mixture into a mixing bowl.

Add the graham cracker crumbs to another shallow bowl.

Dip the widened end of the strawberry in the cream cheese mixture, and then roll it around in the graham cracker crumbs.

Place on a baking sheet and refrigerate for 20 minutes.

YIELD: 16 servings

Laura's Tip

Alternatively, you can use about ⅓ cup (115 g) honey instead of powdered sugar in this recipe.

Tropical Fruit Cups

My kids love fruit cups, but store-bought canned varieties are often filled with high fructose corn syrup. Why buy them when making your own is simple and a lot more nutritious? Feel free to use other fruits such as ripe pears, peaches, or sliced grapes.

3 kiwis

1 cup (175 g) mango chunks

1 cup (165 g) pineapple chunks

1 tablespoon (20 g) honey

Cut the kiwis in half and scoop out flesh. Cut kiwi halves into chunks and place in a medium bowl.

Add mango chunks, pineapple chunks, and honey to the bowl. Toss to coat and refrigerate for one hour or until chilled.

Divide among 6 dessert bowls and serve.

YIELD: 6 servings

Grape Poppers ▶

These are just as fun to eat as they are to make!

48 fresh grapes

1 cup (175 g) white chocolate chips

½ cup (55 g) chopped pecans (may substitute for other nuts or sunflower seeds)

Wash grapes and pat them dry with paper towels. Spear each grape with a lollipop stick.

In a double boiler with 1 to 2 inches (2.5 to 5 cm) of water, melt white chocolate chips over medium heat. Remove from stove and set aside.

Holding the end of the lollipop stick, dip each grape in the melted white chocolate. Allow excess chocolate to drip off into the bowl of melted chocolate.

Immediately dip the chocolate covered end of the grape in the chopped pecans.

Place on parchment-lined baking sheet and refrigerate for 30 minutes or until ready to serve.

YIELD: 48 poppers

- -

KITCHEN NOTE

A microwave may be used to melt the chocolate chips. Refer to the package directions to avoid burning the chocolate.

- -

Strawberry Shortcake Kabobs

This is one of my daughter's favorite ways of eating strawberries—skewered with pieces of cake! The kabobs are the perfect way to use up leftover pound cake and they make a great party treat.

1 pound cake, sliced and cubed

2 pounds (910 g) fresh strawberries

½ cup (88 g) chocolate chips

½ cup (88 g) white chocolate chips

Hull the strawberries and then wash them, patting each dry with paper towels.

Slide pound cake cubes and strawberries onto ice-cream sticks, alternating cake and berries as you go. Set loaded skewers on a parchment-lined baking sheet.

In separate bowls, melt dark and white chocolate chips in your microwave, heating each for 30 seconds, stirring, and then heating again until the chips are completely melted.

Drizzle a little melted dark chocolate and a little melted white chocolate over each of the skewers. Refrigerate for 10 minutes, or until ready to serve.

YIELD: 16 servings

Laura's Tip

Don't want to use a store-bought pound cake? Make my Peaches and Cream Bread (page 86) and slice that instead. The chocolate makes this a special treat, so feel free to omit.

Summer Peach Salad

Sweet and nutritious, this tasty salad is loaded with vitamin C and protein. And, it packs easily in a container, making it great for picnics, lunch, or a snack to go.

1 recipe Peach Salsa (page 79)

1 can (15 ounces, or 425 g) black beans, rinsed and drained

In a large bowl, combine Peach Salsa and black beans.

Season with additional salt, if needed, and refrigerate.

Serve chilled.

YIELD: 6 to 8 servings

Tropical Banana Bites

Kids love finger foods! In this delicious snack, bananas, peanut butter, and coconut provide the perfect combination in one single bite! Those with peanut allergies can easily substitute the peanut with butter, sunflower butter, or soy butter.

⅓ cup (87 g) peanut butter

3 bananas, cut into ½-inch (12 mm) slices

3 tablespoons (15 g) shredded coconut

Working over a parchment-lined baking sheet, spread peanut butter onto a banana slice, sprinkle with shredded coconut, and top with another banana slice. Set on baking sheet.

Repeat with the remaining banana slices.

Refrigerate for 1 hour prior to serving.

YIELD: 3 to 4 servings

Chocolate Banana Pops ▶

Eating a banana has never been this much fun! This is the perfect kitchen activity for kids, so invite them to help make their own treat.

1 cup (175 g) chocolate chips

1 tablespoon (14 g) coconut oil

Assorted toppings for coating bananas, such as crushed homemade cookies, sprinkles, nuts, or shredded coconut

3 bananas, peeled

In a double boiler, melt chocolate chips and coconut oil.

Place each topping in a separate shallow dish.

On a flat surface, cut bananas in half. Push an ice-cream stick through each banana half.

Dip the first banana half in the melted chocolate, allow the excess chocolate to drip from the banana into the bowl, and transfer the banana to a parchment-lined cookie sheet.

Sprinkle a few toppings over the banana. Have fun with this step, mixing and matching toppings as you please.

Repeat the dipping and topping process with the remaining banana halves.

Place coated banana halves in the freezer for 1 hour. Remove from freezer and enjoy!

YIELD: 6 servings

Watermelon Pops

Watermelon is the ultimate summer refreshment fruit, and it's loaded with vitamin A, vitamin C, and potassium. Why not make eating it more fun?

¼ watermelon

Ice-cream sticks

Wash watermelon and use a chef's knife to cut it into 6 triangle-shaped slices, 1-inch (2.5 cm) thick.

Use a paring knife to make a slit in the rind just large enough to fit the ice-cream stick. Repeat for each watermelon slice.

Slide an ice-cream stick into the rind of each melon slice and serve.

YIELD: 6 pieces

Laura's Tip

Refrigerate or freeze your watermelon pops to keep them cool; this makes them an even more refreshing snack on hot days.

Crunchy Berry Salad

Move over traditional fruit salad! This crunchy berry salad packs a lot of the vitamins kids need and parents love. The extra crunch and the creamy texture give this healthy snack the ultimate appeal.

½ cup (115 g) Greek vanilla yogurt

1 mango, peeled and diced

1 cup (170 g) strawberries, diced

1 cup (145 g) blueberries

⅓ cup (37 g) chopped pecans

In a large bowl, combine Greek yogurt with mango, strawberries, and blueberries. Add the pecans and fold to combine.

Refrigerate for 1 hour and serve.

YIELD: 6 servings

Crunchy Apple Cheesecake

Here's a creamy and delicious treat without any of the guilt of eating the real thing.

2 whole-grain rice cakes

3 tablespoons (45 g) Cinnamon-Roll Flavored Cream Cheese (page 72)

1 small apple, peeled and sliced thin

Dash of cinnamon

Spread 1½ tablespoons (22 g) Cinnamon Roll-Flavored Cream Cheese onto each rice cake.

Top with apple slices and sprinkle with cinnamon.

YIELD: 2 servings

Mixed Berry and Banana Fruit Salad

This fruit salad combination is our family's favorite.

2 teaspoons lemon juice

2 bananas, peeled and thickly sliced

2 cups (340 g) strawberries, roughly chopped

¼ cup (31 g) raspberries

1 cup (145 g) blueberries

½ teaspoon lemon zest

1 tablespoon (20 g) honey

In a medium bowl, combine lemon juice and sliced bananas. Gently toss them to combine.

Meanwhile, wash and prep the berries. Toss strawberries into the banana bowl as you chop them.

Add raspberries, blueberries, lemon zest, and honey to the bowl. Gently toss to coat everything with honey.

Cover and chill for 1 hour.

YIELD: 6 servings

Ham and Cheese Apple Wraps

Apples and cheese are a classic combination, but this easy snack takes the pairing to a new level. Sometimes I even pack this for myself as a healthy office snack.

1 apple, sliced

4 ounces (115 g) deli ham, thinly sliced

2 ounces (40 g) cheddar cheese, thinly sliced

Place a slice of apple and a slice of cheese on top of each slice of ham.

Roll the ham around the middle of the apple and serve.

YIELD: 2 servings

Oven-Fried Bananas

When I was a young girl, my grandma used to make these delicious bananas for our afternoon snack. They are melt-in-your-mouth delicious, and this is one recipe I make often. They aren't really "fried," but that's what she used to call them.

2 bananas, halved lengthwise

1 tablespoon (20 g) honey

Cinnamon, for dusting

Preheat the oven to 350°F (180°C).

Place sliced bananas in a glass or ceramic baking dish. Drizzle honey and dust with cinnamon.

Bake 7 to 10 minutes, or until the bananas soften and begin to brown. Serve warm.

YIELD: 4 servings

Laura's Tip

Sprinkle bananas with finely chopped nuts.

◀ Veggie Dipping Jars

These hummus jars are fun to eat, easy to make, and have a lot of snack appeal.

3 tablespoons (10 g) Homemade Hummus (page 74)

1 cup (150 g) raw veggies, such as carrots, peppers, green beans, or snap peas, cut into strips

Spoon hummus into the bottom of an 8-ounce (250 ml) canning jar.

Fill the jar with the raw vegetables of your choice and serve.

YIELD: 1 serving

- -

KITCHEN NOTE

Take these on the go by using plastic freezer jars. You can find them in the canning aisle next to the glass ones or through online retailers.

- -

Laura's Tip

Transport these bite-size snacks upright in a cupcake carrier.

Italian Flag Bites

When my daughter's class was learning about Italy, it was her (my) turn to bring a savory treat. These little bites are fresh and the perfect little snack.

8 ounces (225 g) cream cheese, softened

1 tablespoon (15 g) plain yogurt

1 teaspoon Italian seasoning

3 cucumbers, peeled and sliced

12 cherry tomatoes, halved

In the bowl of a food processor, combine cream cheese, yogurt, and Italian seasoning. Transfer creamy mix to a zip-top bag and cut the tip off a corner to use as a piping bag.

Pipe about 2 teaspoons of creamy mix onto each cucumber slice. Top each with a cherry tomato half and arrange on a plate.

Refrigerate for 30 minutes before serving.

YIELD: 24 flag bites

Mediterranean Cucumber Cups

My mom made these as an appetizer for a party and I devoured half the tray. Now, I make the Mediterranean salad and have it ready to stuff into cucumbers for a healthy and fresh snack.

½ small red onion, finely chopped

½ red bell pepper, finely chopped

1 ripe tomato, seeded and finely chopped

2 tablespoons (20 g) black olives, pitted and chopped

¾ teaspoon dried oregano

⅛ cup (19 g) fresh feta, crumbled

¼ cup (15 g) fresh parsley, chopped

Juice of 1 lemon

1 teaspoon lemon zest

1 tablespoon (15 ml) extra virgin olive oil

¼ teaspoon salt

¼ teaspoon pepper

2 large cucumbers

In a large mixing bowl, combine onion, bell pepper, tomato, black olives, oregano, feta, parsley, lemon juice and zest, and olive oil. Season to taste with salt and pepper.

Peel cucumbers and trim the ends. Cut cucumbers into 1-inch (2.5 cm) thick pieces. With a melon baller or a knife, scoop out the center, leaving a ⅛-inch (3 mm) base.

Fill each cucumber cup with about 1 tablespoon (15 g) of the Mediterranean salad. Refrigerate for 20 minutes and serve.

YIELD: 4 to 6 servings

Chocolate Covered ▶ Kiwi Pops

For the kids who complain about the tiny seeds in kiwi, this recipe is for you. This is what I call real fruit lollypops.

½ cup (88 g) semisweet chocolate chips

½ teaspoon coconut oil

2 kiwis, peeled and sliced

Melt chocolate and coconut oil in a double boiler. For microwave melting, follow the directions on the chips package and stir frequently to prevent the chocolate from burning.

Insert the ice-cream sticks into the kiwi slices just far enough to hold the fruit without piercing through the other end.

Dip the kiwi slices into the melted chocolate to cover as desired, and hold over wax paper or standing up in an egg carton, until chocolate is cooled.

Once chocolate sets, enjoy immediately.

YIELD: 4 to 6 servings

Tuna Salad Cucumber Cups

I always keep a simple tuna salad in the fridge for quick and easy snacking. This protein-rich snack is one we often eat late in the evening, when after school activities keep us out past our regular dinnertime.

10 ounces (280 g) tuna, packed in water, drained

2 tablespoons (30 g) plain Greek yogurt

½ teaspoon yellow mustard

Salt and pepper, to taste

2 cucumbers

In a medium mixing bowl, combine tuna, Greek yogurt, and mustard with a fork. Season to taste with salt and pepper.

Peel the cucumbers and trim off the ends. Cut cucumbers into 1-inch (2.5 cm) thick pieces. With a melon baller or a knife, scoop out the center, leaving a ⅛-inch (3 mm) base.

Fill each cucumber cup with about 1 tablespoon (11 g) of the tuna salad. Refrigerate for 20 minutes before serving.

YIELD: 3 to 4 servings

Caprese Skewers

"Skewer anything and they'll eat it!" said my friend Christine. I put her claim to the test with this snack, which is basically my favorite salad on a stick.

10 grape or cherry tomatoes, halved

8 ounces (225 g) fresh mozzarella, cut into 20 cubes

Fresh basil leaves

½ cup (130 g) Homemade Pesto (page 76)

Using a flexible skewer, poke through a tomato, a mozzarella cube, some basil leaves, another mozzarella cube, and another tomato.

Repeat process with remaining ingredients. Serve with a side of fresh pesto for dipping.

YIELD: 10 skewers

Laura's Tip

Skip the cubing by purchasing bite-size mozzarella balls. They are fresh, delicious, and just as tasty!

Easy Strawberry Jam

During berry season, I purchase a lot of fresh strawberries on sale and freeze them for smoothies. Sometimes I find a bag or two that have been in the back of my freezer for a bit too long. Instead of tossing them out, I repurpose them into an easy-to-make jam. This jam is the perfect filling for our crêpes and toaster pastries.

6 cups (780 g) strawberries, diced

Juice of 1 lemon

1 cup (340 g) honey

Place all of the ingredients into a 5-quart (4.7 L) pot and bring it to a boil over medium to high heat. Stir occasionally, so the jam doesn't burn.

Lower heat to a simmer and cook for about 10 minutes. Berry jam will begin to thicken.

With a spoon, test for thickness, (it should be the consistency of runny pudding) and turn off heat. Berries will finish cooking during the canning process.

Spoon hot jam into sterilized canning jars, and cover with sterilized lids and rings. Do not tighten rings completely.

Carefully lower jars into a canner or large stock pot filled with boiling water. Process for 10 minutes.

Use a jar lifter to carefully remove each jar from pot and set on a clean towel on the counter to cool.

As jars cool to room temperature, the lids will pop, indicating that they are sealed. You can test each seal by pressing down on the center of the lid; if it "gives" and makes a popping sound, it is not sealed. Store any jars with lids that do not seal within several hours in the refrigerator and use within 2 to 3 weeks.

YIELD: 1½ pints (960 g)

- -

KITCHEN NOTE

You can substitute sugar for the honey in this recipe.

- -

CHAPTER 3

NO-BAKE BITES AND DIPS

During the summer, I give my oven a much-needed rest from nine months of baking and focus on easy, no-bake snacks. This is easier than you'd think. This chapter includes many recipes for delicious snack bars and nutritious cookies that require only mixing the ingredients, shaping the dough into bars or bites, and chilling until firm.

Dips provide another no-bake option. They are also my solution to getting my kids to try new veggies and eat more of them between meals. I hope they make eating veggies more fun at your house as well.

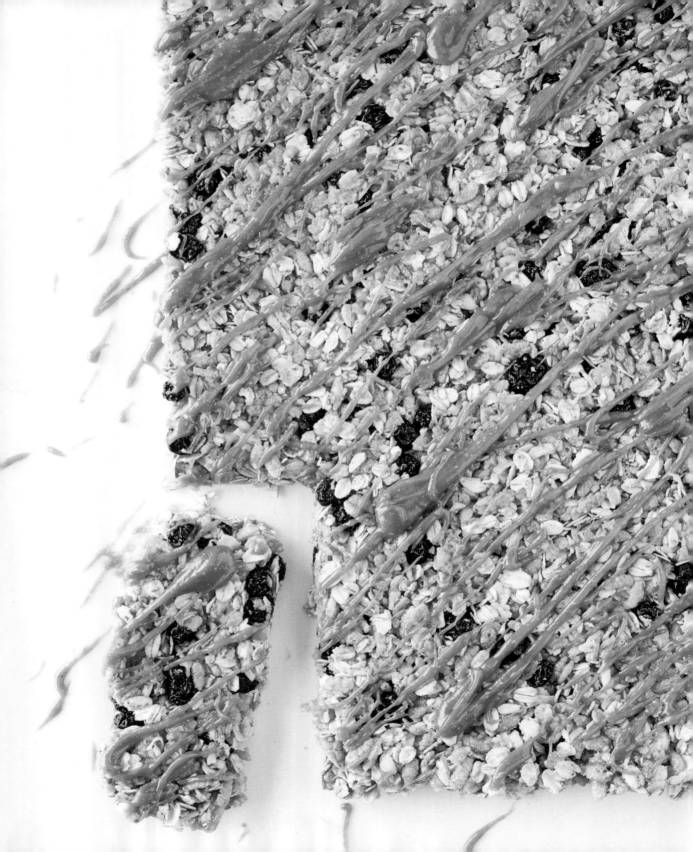

Blueberry Vanilla Granola Bars

Basic, delicious, and nutritious, these bars are sure to become a favorite in your household. Of course the glaze is optional—and they are just as good without it!.

For the bars:

2 cups (160 g) rolled oats

1½ cups (40 g) rice cereal

¼ cup (20 g) shredded unsweetened coconut

¼ cup (30 g) walnuts, chopped

1 tablespoon (12 g) ground flax meal

¼ teaspoon salt

½ cup (130 g) almond butter

½ cup (170 g) honey

1 teaspoon vanilla extract

¾ cup (110 g) dried blueberries

For the glaze:

1 tablespoon (16 g) almond butter (peanut will work)

2 teaspoons (10 ml) melted coconut oil

1 tablespoon (15 ml) cold pure maple syrup

½ teaspoon vanilla extract

TO MAKE THE BARS: Line a 9 × 13-inch (23 × 33 cm) pan with parchment paper, allowing an inch (2.5 cm) of the paper to extend above the sides of the pan.

In a large bowl combine the oats, rice cereal, coconut, walnuts, flax meal, and salt.

In a small microwave-safe bowl combine almond butter and honey. Microwave for 30 seconds, or until the mixture is warm and pourable. Add the vanilla and mix well.

Pour the honey mixture into the dry oat mixture and mix until everything is evenly combined. Add the blueberries and fold a few times to distribute.

Transfer the granola bar mixture into the prepared pan and firmly press down until tightly packed. Cover with plastic wrap and place in the freezer for 1 hour.

TO MAKE THE GLAZE: In a microwave-safe bowl, heat the almond butter for 30 seconds. Add the coconut oil and mix until thoroughly combined. Add the cold maple syrup and vanilla and whisk until smooth.

Remove bars from freezer, uncover, and drizzle maple glaze over pressed bars. Allow glaze to cool completely.

To remove the bars from the pan, lift the parchment paper.

Place the bars on a cutting board, with the parchment side up. Peel off the parchment paper and cut the granola into 12 bars.

Store in an airtight container at room temperature for up to 1 week.

YIELD: 12 granola bars

Winnie-the-Pooh Snacks

The first time I made these snacks, my daughter Sofia, who was 4 at the time, said, "Mommy, I think Winnie the Pooh would love these since he likes honey so much!" This has been a favorite recipe in our house ever since.

½ cup (112 g) creamy almond butter

¼ cup (85 g) honey

½ teaspoon vanilla extract

⅓ cup (27 g) unsweetened shredded coconut

⅓ cup (42 g) coconut flour

½ teaspoon cinnamon

In a medium bowl, combine almond butter, honey, vanilla, shredded coconut, coconut flour, and cinnamon. Mix all ingredients until they form a crumbly, sticky dough.

Scoop out tablespoon-size portions and roll into balls.

Place on a plate and serve immediately or refrigerate in an airtight container for up to 3 days.

YIELD: 18 bite-size snacks

- -

KITCHEN NOTE

Not all almond butters have the same consistency, they tend to vary by brand. If the mixture is too sticky, add 1 tablespoon (8 g) coconut flour, mix and refrigerate for 15 minutes. If it's too dry, add additional honey or 1 teaspoon water and combine.

- -

Brown Rice Krispy Treats ▷

When my kids learned that the classic treat was sold in single-serve packages at the grocery store, I added this recipe to my list of homemade snacks. Better yet, I improved the quality of the classic recipe by ditching the marshmallows and adding protein-rich peanut butter.

1 box (10 ounces, or 284 g) brown rice cereal

1¾ cups (595 g) brown rice syrup

Pinch of salt

¾ cup (195 g) peanut butter

½ cup (90 g) semisweet or nondairy chocolate chips

Pour the rice cereal into a large bowl.

Heat the syrup with a pinch of salt in a saucepan over low heat. When the rice syrup liquefies, add the peanut butter and stir well until combined. Pour over the rice cereal. Mix well.

Once the cereal mixture has cooled, stir in the chocolate chips. Pour the mixture into a 9-inch (23 cm) square baking dish. Let cool for 1 hour before cutting into bars.

YIELD: 16 servings

Laura's Tip

You can also use almond butter for this recipe. To make these nut free, use soy or sunflower seed butter.

◄ Drop Cookies

One hot summer day, I called my friend Alison, desperate for a cookie recipe that did not require turning on the oven. She shared this recipe while saying, "They aren't the prettiest cookies, but they are delicious." She was right.

⅓ cup (75 g) butter

⅓ cup (115 g) honey

⅓ cup (80 ml) milk

¾ cup (195 g) creamy peanut butter

1 teaspoon pure vanilla extract

Pinch of salt

2 cups (160 g) quick cooking oats

¾ cup (131 g) vegan semisweet chocolate chips

In a medium saucepan, melt butter over medium heat. Add honey and milk. Cook, stirring until the mixture comes to a boil. Continue stirring for 1 to 2 minutes, or until the honey dissolves.

Remove the saucepan from the heat. Add the peanut butter, vanilla, and salt, stirring until well blended. Add the oats and chocolate chips and stir until completely combined.

Drop by heaping tablespoon-size scoops onto parchment paper. Leave at room temperature until firm, about 20 minutes.

YIELD: About 24 cookies

Chocolate Peanut Butter Pretzel Haystacks

Who can resist a crunchy chocolate peanut butter treat? This satisfying snack combines everyone's favorite flavors—it's salty and sweet with the richness of chocolate.

2 cups (350 g) semisweet chocolate chips

½ cup (130 g) peanut butter

3 cups (175 g) pretzel sticks, coarsely broken

½ cup (73 g) peanuts, coarsely chopped

Line 2 baking sheets with waxed paper.

In a large microwave-safe bowl, heat the chocolate chips and peanut butter, stirring every 20 seconds, for about 1 minute or until fully melted.

Add pretzel sticks and peanuts and stir until everything is well coated.

Drop full tablespoon-sized scoops of the mixture onto waxed paper. Refrigerate until the chocolate is firm.

YIELD: Approximately 4 dozen haystacks

Oatmeal Raisin Cookie Dough Bites ▶

Sometimes in the summer, when I don't want to turn on the oven, I make these to satisfy our love for oatmeal raisin cookies.

½ cup (130 g) creamy raw almond butter

¼ cup (85 g) raw honey or maple syrup

1 teaspoon vanilla extract

¼ cup (31 g) coconut flour

3 tablespoons (15 g) quick oats

2 tablespoons (14 g) ground flaxseed

¼ teaspoon cinnamon

¼ teaspoon sea salt

¼ cup (35 g) raisins

In a large bowl, mix together nut butter, honey (or maple syrup) and vanilla until creamy and well blended.

In a separate bowl, combine the coconut flour, quick oats, ground flaxseed, cinnamon, and sea salt. Add dry ingredients to the wet and mix well to combine (I like to use a wooden spoon). Fold in the raisins.

Use your hands to knead the dough. If the dough is too wet, add a bit more coconut flour. If it's too dry and doesn't hold together well, knead in 1 or 2 teaspoons water.

Scoop out tablespoon-size portions and roll into 1-inch (2.5 cm) balls using your hands to create a bite-size treat.

Refrigerate for 30 minutes and enjoy.

YIELD: 18 bites

Chocolate Brownie Energy Bites ▶

These are the only brownie bites I don't feel guilty eating at four o'clock in the afternoon. The raisins add fiber while the cashews add protein, making this a satisfying and nutritious snack.

1 cup (145 g) raisins, packed

1 cup (120 g) cashews

¼ cup (20 g) cocoa powder

1 teaspoon vanilla extract

¼ teaspoon salt

Pinch of cinnamon

Place raisins in a medium bowl and cover with hot water. Soak for 5 minutes to soften then drain.

Add raisins and all remaining ingredients into a food processor and pulse until mixture is the consistency of sand. Remove blade from the unit.

Using your hands, scoop out dough and form into balls on the palms of your hands.

Chill for 30 minutes and enjoy. Store in an airtight container in the fridge for up to 1 week.

YIELD: 18 bites

Chocolate Banana Mini Pretzelwiches

If my son could eat these every day, I'm pretty sure he would! Feel free to substitute gluten-free pretzels if anyone in your family has gluten sensitivities.

1 cup (175 g) chocolate chips

1 teaspoon coconut oil

2 medium bananas, sliced

24 mini pretzels

Melt chocolate chips and coconut oil in a double boiler filled with 1 to 2 inches (2.5 to 5 cm) of water. Once melted, turn off the heat.

Sandwich one banana slice between two mini pretzels.

Dip the banana pretzelwich into the melted chocolate and place it on a parchment-covered baking tray.

Repeat the sandwich and dipping process with all remaining banana slices and refrigerate for 10 minutes.

Store in an airtight container and refrigerate for up to 2 days.

YIELD: 12 to 14 pieces

Laura's Tip

Skip the chocolate and sandwich the banana slices with nut butter between the pretzels.

Bananas Gone Nuts!

For times when bananas are too green to eat alone, this recipe comes to the rescue every time! Not only is it delicious, this snack is loaded with potassium and protein.

3 bananas, peeled

⅓ cup (87 g) peanut butter

⅓ cup (48 g) chopped peanuts

Cut bananas in half and insert an ice-cream stick through the middle.

Warm peanut butter for 10 to 15 seconds in the microwave to soften. Coat bananas with peanut butter and roll in crushed peanuts.

YIELD: 6 servings

Monkey Kisses

After tasting this recipe, my son Alex, who was 4 at the time, gave this review: "Mom, bananas are way better with chocolate." I have to agree with that one.

3 bananas, peeled

½ cup (130 g) Homemade Chocolate Hazelnut Spread (page 205)

⅓ cup (27 g) shredded coconut

Slice bananas into ½-inch (3 mm) slices. Spread Homemade Chocolate Hazelnut Spread over each banana slice and sprinkle with shredded coconut.

You may choose to refrigerate for 10 minutes before serving to firm up the hazelnut spread, but it's not necessary.

YIELD: 6 servings

Birthday Cake Bites

Not wanting to turn on the oven during the middle of a hot summer, I made these cake bites to appease my kids, who were begging for cupcakes.

¼ cup (65 g) creamy cashew butter

¼ cup (85 g) maple syrup or honey

2 teaspoons (10 ml) vanilla extract

¼ teaspoon butter extract

1 tablespoon (15 ml) water

¼ cup (31 g) plus 2 tablespoons (16 g) coconut flour

3 tablespoons (25 g) oat flour

¼ teaspoon salt

In a large bowl, mix together cashew butter, maple syrup (or honey), vanilla, butter extract, and water until creamy and well combined.

In a small bowl, combine coconut flour, oat flour, and salt.

Add dry ingredients to the wet and mix thoroughly with a fork to combine. When the fork no longer does the trick, begin to knead the thick dough with your hands.

Scoop out tablespoon-size portions and roll into 1-inch (2.5 cm) balls.

Refrigerate for 30 minutes and serve.

YIELD: 18 bites

- - - - - - - - - - - - - - - - - - - -

KITCHEN NOTE

If the "dough" is too wet, add 1 additional teaspoon of coconut flour. Not all cashew butters have the same consistency so you might have to adjust.

- - - - - - - - - - - - - - - - - - - -

Chocolate Strawberry Shortcakes

I make these as a special treat when I don't have enough berries to make some of our other favorite fruity snacks.

⅓ cup (58 g) chocolate chips

1 teaspoon coconut oil

20 vanilla wafers

5 strawberries, halved

⅓ cup (67 g) whipped cream cheese

In a double boiler, melt chocolate chips and coconut oil.

Meanwhile, spread about a teaspoon of cream cheese onto each wafer. Place a half of a strawberry on ten of the wafers and top each with another wafer.

Carefully dip each wafer and strawberry sandwich into the melted chocolate, allowing excess to drip off into the pan. Place on a parchment-lined baking sheet and refrigerate for 15 minutes or until set.

YIELD: 10 strawberry shortcakes

Laura's Tip

Double the recipe and make these the night before a party. I promise they will be a huge crowdpleaser!

Caramel Cheesecake Apple Dip

When my daughter began eating apple slices at a birthday party dipped in the mysterious caramel dip that came with the fruit tray, I knew I had to re-create the recipe with ingredients I could pronounce.

½ cup (130 g) peanut butter

½ cup (88 g) caramel chips

8 ounces (225 g) cream cheese, chilled

1 cup (230 g) plain Greek yogurt

¼ teaspoon cinnamon

2 medium apples, sliced for serving

1 cup (72 g) crushed graham crackers

In a small, microwave-safe bowl, heat caramel chips and peanut butter in 15-second increments, stopping to mix well between each cycle. Set aside to cool.

In the bowl of a food processor, mix cream cheese and Greek yogurt until thoroughly combined. Add cooled caramel peanut butter mixture, cinnamon, and pulse to combine.

Transfer the dip to a serving dish. Refrigerate for 1 hour prior to serving.

Serve with apple slices and a small dish of broken graham crackers. Dip apple slices into caramel cheesecake dip then into graham cracker crumbs. Refrigerate unused cheesecake dip in an airtight container for up to 1 week.

YIELD: 10 servings

Lemonade Stand Fruit Dip

My friend Alison's boys loved the Dreamsicle Fruit Dip (at right) so much, she created a tangier version. It's hard to say no to fruit dipped in this!

6 ounces (170 g) vanilla Greek yogurt

4 ounces (115 g) cream cheese, softened

½ cup (142 g) frozen lemonade concentrate

In a medium bowl, mix yogurt, cream cheese, and lemonade concentrate. Mix until thoroughly combined and refrigerate until ready to serve.

YIELD: Approximately 2 cups (450 g)

Laura's Tip

It's easy to over-indulge in these sweet dips, so I make single-serve portions by measuring out in 1 to 2 tablespoons (15 to 28 g) into small single-serve containers.

Dreamsicle Fruit Dip ▶

My kids go nuts over this dip. It's sweet, and I serve it as a treat with a generous serving of fruits such as pineapple, apples, orange slices, or grapes.

6 ounces (170 g) vanilla Greek yogurt

4 ounces (115 g) cream cheese, softened

½ cup (142 g) frozen orange juice concentrate

In a medium bowl, mix yogurt, cream cheese, and orange juice concentrate. Mix until thoroughly combined and refrigerate until ready to serve.

YIELD: Approximately 2 cups (450 g)

Maple Cinnamon Dip

Re-creating the expensive apple platter from the grocery store is easy to do with real ingredients. Best of all, this dip wins the taste test hands down.

¼ cup (60 g) cream cheese

6 ounces (170 g) vanilla yogurt

2 teaspoons maple syrup

½ teaspoon cinnamon

Baked Cinnamon Tortilla Chips (page 125), for serving

Fresh fruit, for serving

In a small bowl, mix the cream cheese, yogurt, sugar and cinnamon until smooth.

Serve with Baked Cinnamon Tortilla Chips (page 125) and fruit.

YIELD: Approximately 1½ cups (245 g)

Blueberry Lemon–Flavored Cream Cheese

My husband spreads this on his bagel and calls it a bagel-muffin. I absolutely love the lemon zest flavor that shines through the creamy, sweet taste of the blueberries.

8 ounces (225 g) cream cheese, softened

½ cup (75 g) blueberries

1 teaspoon lemon zest

In a food processor or blender, combine softened cream cheese, blueberries, and lemon zest. Process until smooth and thoroughly mixed.

Store in an airtight container in the refrigerator for up to a week.

YIELD: 1¼ cups (290 g)

Cinnamon Roll–Flavored Cream Cheese

My family loves to spread this over a hearty whole-wheat bagel, but it would be great on cinnamon raisin bagel as well.

4 ounces (115 g) cream cheese, softened

1 tablespoon (15 g) brown sugar

1 teaspoon cinnamon

⅛ teaspoon nutmeg

In a medium mixing bowl, whip the cream cheese until softened and fluffy. Add brown sugar, cinnamon, and nutmeg, fold to combine.

Refrigerate in an airtight container for up to a week.

YIELD: Approximately ⅓ cup (130 g)

Peaches-and-Cream-Flavored Cream Cheese

I swear this creamy, delicious spread tastes just like summer. It's great inside a homemade crêpe (page 171) or spread on a toasted bagel.

8 ounces (225 g) cream cheese, softened

½ cup (125 g) frozen peaches, thawed

In a food processor or blender, combine softened cream cheese and peaches. Process until smooth and thoroughly mixed.

Refrigerate in an airtight container for up to a week.

YIELD: 1¼ cups (350 g)

Savory Herb-Flavored Cream Cheese

This is the perfect base for smoked salmon or salty meats over crackers, crostini, rye crisps, and more!

4 ounces (115 g) cream cheese, softened

1 scallion, finely chopped

2 teaspoons minced parsley

¼ teaspoon black pepper

In a food processor or blender, combine softened cream cheese and herbs. Process until smooth and thoroughly mixed.

Refrigerate in an airtight container for up to a week.

YIELD: Approximately ⅓ cup (120 g)

Homemade Hummus

Nobody in my family makes hummus like my dad, Yanni. His smooth and creamy version is our favorite for spreading or dipping just about anything!

2 cans (4 ounces, or 398 g each) chickpeas, drained and rinsed

3 tablespoons (45 ml) lemon juice

2 tablespoons (30 g) tahini

2 tablespoons (30 ml) olive oil

2 teaspoons ground cumin

1 to 2 garlic cloves

1 to 1¼ cups (235 to 285 ml) water

Salt and ground pepper to taste

In a food processor or blender, combine chickpeas, lemon juice, tahini, oil, cumin, and garlic. Mix for one minute.

Begin to thin with water, adding it in slowly until you reach the thickness or consistency you desire. Season with salt and pepper.

Refrigerate in an airtight container for up to 1 week.

YIELD: 2½ cups (490 g)

Edamame Hummus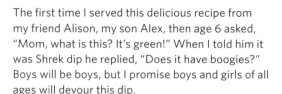

The first time I served this delicious recipe from my friend Alison, my son Alex, then age 6 asked, "Mom, what is this? It's green!" When I told him it was Shrek dip he replied, "Does it have boogies?" Boys will be boys, but I promise boys and girls of all ages will devour this dip.

1½ cups (225 g) frozen shelled edamame (soy beans)

2 tablespoons (30 g) tahini

¼ cup (60 ml) water

3 tablespoons (45 ml) lemon juice, about 1 lemon

2 teaspoons soy sauce

1 clove garlic, grated or minced

¾ teaspoon kosher salt

½ teaspoon cumin

¼ teaspoon ground coriander

3 tablespoons (45 ml) olive oil

1 tablespoon (4 g) fresh, flat leaf parsley, finely chopped

Boil edamame in salted water for 4 to 5 minutes, or microwave, covered for 2 to 3 minutes.

In a food processor, purée the edamame, tahini, water, lemon juice, soy sauce, garlic, salt, cumin, and coriander until smooth. Then drizzle in olive oil, mixing until fully combined.

Transfer to a medium bowl and fold in parsley.

YIELD: 4 servings

Fresh Herb Yogurt Dip

My friend Alison gave me this recipe so I could use all of the veggies that I pick up from the farmers' market each week. So far, so good!

1 cup (230 g) whole milk Greek yogurt

1 teaspoon extra-virgin olive oil

2 teaspoons lemon juice

1 tablespoon (3 g) fresh chives, chopped

2 tablespoons (8 g) fresh parsley, chopped

2 cloves garlic, minced

¼ teaspoon sea salt

⅛ teaspoon freshly ground black pepper

Place all the ingredients in a medium bowl and stir until thoroughly combined.

Enjoy immediately or refrigerate, storing in an airtight container, for up to 3 days.

YIELD: 4 to 6 servings

Homemade Pesto

At any given time, you'll find a jar of this delicious and flavorful sauce in my fridge. A good pesto sauce is so versatile and easy to make that it can be the basis of a delicious dip, snack, and even a meal! For a nut-free option, substitute sunflower or pumpkin seeds for walnuts.

2 cups (80 g) fresh basil

¼ cup (25 g) Parmesan cheese, grated

¼ cup (25 g) walnuts

1 garlic clove

½ teaspoon salt

¼ cup (60 ml) olive oil

Add all ingredients into a food processor and purée until smooth.

YIELD: 1 cup (260 mg)

Laura's Tip

To make a creamy dip, simply add ¾ cup (175 g) plain Greek yogurt to ¼ cup (65 g) pesto.

Eggplant Dip

When you find eggplant in your farmer share box for a few weeks in a row, you begin to get creative with recipes. This dip has become a family favorite.

1 large eggplant

2 teaspoons olive oil

¼ teaspoon salt

2 cloves garlic, grated

2 to 3 tablespoons (30 to 45 ml) fresh lemon juice

¼ cup (60 g) tahini

Preheat the oven to 425°F (220°C).

Cut the eggplant in half lengthwise, brush the cut side with olive oil, and sprinkle with salt. Roast for 45 minutes to 1 hour, or until the eggplant is very soft and blackened around the edges. Remove from the oven and allow to cool.

Using a spoon, scoop the eggplant meat away from the skin. Place roasted eggplant inside a strainer and press out any moisture. Transfer to a food processor.

Use a microplane to grate the garlic directly over the bowl of the food processor, and then add lemon juice and tahini.

Pulse a few times to combine and the let it run until smooth. Season with salt and pepper to taste.

YIELD: Approximately 1½ cups (338 g)

KITCHEN NOTE
Refrigerate any leftovers in a covered container for up to five days.

Blue Cheese Yogurt Dip

Growing up, my aunt made this blue cheese dip nearly every time I went to play with my cousins. It's still my favorite dip for raw veggies.

4 ounces (115 g) blue cheese, crumbled

1½ cups (345 g) plain yogurt

In a medium bowl, combine blue cheese and yogurt.

Refrigerate for at least 1 hour before serving.

YIELD: Approximately 2 cups (460 g)

Yanni's Greek Dip

I love going over to my parents' house and finding a bowl of this traditional Greek dip in their fridge. It's perfect with raw veggies or on pitas.

1 cucumber, peeled

1 garlic clove

1 cup (230 g) plain yogurt

½ teaspoon salt

½ teaspoon lemon juice

¼ teaspoon dried dill

Place a grater inside a medium bowl. Grate cucumber and garlic clove into the bowl.

Add plain yogurt, salt, lemon juice, and dill to the cucumber and garlic.

Combine all ingredients well and refrigerate for at least 1 hour before serving.

YIELD: 4 servings

Peach Salsa

This is our salsa of choice in the summer, when fragrant, ripe peaches are available everywhere. The sweetness of the peaches cuts the acidity of the tomatoes to create the perfect, tangy dip for chips.

4 medium peaches, peeled, pitted, and diced

1 pint (300 g) yellow or red tomatoes, quartered

1 small jalapeño, ribs removed, deseeded, chopped

1 shallot, chopped

3 tablespoons (3 g) cilantro, chopped

3 tablespoons (45 ml) lime juice

1½ tablespoons (30 g) honey

1½ tablespoons (22 ml) extra-virgin olive oil

½ teaspoon salt

In a large bowl mix together peaches, tomatoes, jalapeño, shallot, and cilantro. Set aside.

In a small separate bowl combine lime juice, honey, and olive oil and whisk together until the honey is dissolved.

Pour lime mixture over peaches and toss to combine. Season with salt and stir.

YIELD: 8 servings

- -

KITCHEN NOTE

Make this salsa year-round using about 1½ cups (375 g) frozen peaches.

- -

Baked Hummus and Spinach Dip

Here is a little twist on the traditional spinach dip that's just as good, but with a lot more protein and overall nutritional value.

1 recipe Homemade Hummus (page 74)

2 cups (60 g) fresh spinach

1¼ cups (150 g) shredded white cheddar cheese, divided

2 teaspoons creole or Italian seasoning

1 batch Homemade Tortilla Chips (page 121)

Prepare Homemade Hummus according to directions on page 74.

Preheat the oven to 375°F (190°C).

On a cutting board, chop spinach by hand into fine shreds.

In a 9 × 9-inch (23 × 23 cm) baking dish, combine hummus, spinach, ¾ cup (90 g) shredded cheese, and creole seasoning. Top with remaining cheese.

Bake for 20 to 25 minutes until cheese is melted and hummus is hot.

Serve with Homemade Tortilla Chips (page 121).

YIELD: 8 servings

CHAPTER 4

BAKED BITES

My grandmother had homemade coffee cake on the kitchen counter at all times. It was everyone's favorite. She had a basic recipe, and then she would change it up using whatever fresh fruits were in season. The Peaches and Cream Bread (page 86) is my version of her cake.

If you love the smell of fresh-baked goods as they rise in the oven, then this chapter is for you!

Coffee Shop Blueberry Cake

For two years, my oldest two kids and I would stop at a Starbucks and buy a coffee, two milks, and two slices of blueberry cake to share while we passed the time waiting for their after-school activities to start. One day I realized how much I was spending on this guilty pleasure and decided to make my own. This recipe yields a large pan, so I like to freeze individual portions for future portable treats.

2 cups (274 g) whole-wheat pastry flour	¾ cup (175 g) plain Greek yogurt
2⅓ cups (292 g) all-purpose flour, divided	½ cup (112 g) butter, softened
1¾ cups (350 g) sugar, divided	5 tablespoons (70 g) butter, chilled
5 teaspoons (23 g) baking powder	2 eggs
1½ teaspoons salt	2 teaspoons vanilla extract
1½ cups (255 ml) milk	3 cups (435 g) blueberries

Preheat the oven to 350°F (180°C) and place baking rack in the middle of the oven. Grease a 9 × 13-inch (23 × 33 cm) baking pan.

In a large mixing bowl or in the bowl of your stand mixer, combine the whole-wheat flour, 2 cups (250 g) all-purpose flour, 1¼ cups (250 g) sugar, baking powder, and salt. Give it a quick mix.

To the dry mix add milk, Greek yogurt, ½ cup (112 g) of softened butter, eggs, and vanilla. Mix on low speed until combined and there are no visible clumps. The batter will be thick.

Gently fold in blueberries with a spatula.

Pour mixture into the greased baking pan.

In a small bowl, mix together the remaining ⅓ cup (42 g) flour and ½ cup (100 g) of sugar.

Cube cold butter and place inside the flour mixture. Create a fine crumble as you mix it with a fork or with your hands. Distribute crumble mixture over the batter.

Bake for 50 to 65 minutes, or until a toothpick inserted into the center of the pan comes out clean. Remove from oven and allow cake to cool to room temperature before serving.

YIELD: 12 servings

KITCHEN NOTE

You may substitute the sugar in the cake with 1 cup (340 g) honey. You'll need ½ cup (100 g) of sugar for the topping. While you can use regular whole-wheat flour instead of pastry flour, I prefer the finer grind for this recipe. It yields a softer cake.

Laura's Tip

I love adding 1 to 2 teaspoons of lemon zest into the wet batter for a little extra flavor.

Carrot Cake Overnight Scones

I'm known among my friends for my love of scones. With this recipe, I combined my favorite cake with the portability of a scone.

3 cups (375 g) all-purpose flour

½ cup (100 g) plus 3 tablespoons (40 g) sugar, divided

2 tablespoons (28 g) baking powder

½ teaspoon salt

½ teaspoon cinnamon

⅓ teaspoon nutmeg

2 cups (475 ml) heavy cream or half and half

½ cup (55 g) grated carrots

½ cup (60 g) chopped walnuts

½ cup (75 g) golden raisins

2 tablespoons (30 ml) milk

Line a baking sheet with parchment paper.

Sift the flour and add to a mixing bowl along with ½ cup (100 g) sugar, baking powder, salt, cinnamon, and nutmeg. Make a well in the center of the flour mixture (or a volcano, as my son likes to call it).

Add the cream to the well and mix with a wooden spoon or using your hands until the batter is evenly moistened. The dough will be a bit sticky.

Add shredded carrots, walnuts, and raisins to the scone batter. Fold over a few times to make sure the ingredients are evenly distributed.

Using your hands, shape the dough into twelve 2-inch (5 cm) round scones and place them onto the baking sheet. Place the baking sheet in the freezer for a couple of hours or overnight, until the dough is frozen.

Preheat the oven to 350°F (180°C). Remove the baking sheet from freezer and let the scones thaw for about 5 minutes. If you are baking all 12 scones you will need to divide the scones between two cookie sheets, as they will expand while baking. Otherwise, leave the ones you don't need in the freezer for another day.

Brush the scones with milk and sprinkle with the additional 3 tablespoons (40 g) of reserved sugar.

Bake the scones for 30 to 40 minutes, or until golden brown. Allow scones to cool on the baking sheet for a few minutes, and then transfer to a wire rack to continue cooling.

Serve the scones warm, or at room temperature. Enjoy the baked scones the same day they are made, or freeze for up to 4 weeks.

YIELD: 12 scones

KITCHEN NOTE

To make this recipe with whole-wheat flour, substitute 1½ cups (188 g) whole-wheat flour for half of the all-purpose flour and add an additional ½ teaspoon baking powder.

Basic Granola Bars

This recipe has become a staple in my household since my friend Alison shared it with me years ago. The mix-ins allow you to create neverending variations of the recipe.

1⅔ cups (133 g) rolled oats

1 cup (39 g) rice cereal

½ cup (115 g) brown sugar

⅓ cup (33 g) oat flour

½ teaspoon salt

¼ teaspoon cinnamon

2 cups (190 to 240 g) total mix-ins (see suggestions at right)

⅓ cup (86 g) peanut butter

6 tablespoons (90 ml) melted butter

1 teaspoon vanilla extract

¼ cup (85 g) honey

1 tablespoon (15 ml) water

Mix-in Ideas (2 cups [190 to 240 g] total):

Raisins

Dried blueberries

Dried cherries

Dried cranberries

Dried apricots

Dates

Walnuts

Chocolate chips

Preheat the oven to 350°F (180°C). Line a 9 × 9 inch (23 × 23 cm) pan with parchment paper.

In a large bowl, combine rolled oats, rice cereal, brown sugar, oat flour, salt, cinnamon. Add in 2 cups (190 to 240 g) total of your mix-ins and combine.

In a medium bowl, whisk together peanut butter, butter, vanilla, honey, and water.

Add wet mixture to the dry mixture, stirring until everything is thoroughly combined into a crumbly wet mixture. Spread into the prepared pan, pressing firmly.

Bake for 30 to 40 minutes or until golden brown along the edges. These will still be soft when they come out of the oven, almost like they are under baked. Keep the bars inside the pan until they've completely cooled.

Once the bars have cooled, cut into squares. If they are too crumbly, refrigerate for 30 minutes before cutting into squares.

YIELD: 12 to 16 servings

Magic Banana Cookies

Apparently these cookies were an Internet sensation way before my friend Jennifer emailed me the recipe. I call them magic cookies because somehow they hold together with minimal ingredients.

2 large ripe bananas

1 cup (80 g) old fashioned oats

¼ cup (44 g) chocolate chips

Preheat the oven to 350°F (180°C). Line a baking sheet with parchment paper.

In the bowl of a food processor, blend bananas and oats until bananas are smooth but you can still see the oats. Add chocolate chips and mix with a spoon.

Scoop out batter using a 2-tablespoon (28 g) cookie dough scoop and place each scoop onto the parchment paper.

Bake for 12 to 15 minutes, or until tops are golden.

YIELD: 12 cookies

Laura's Tip

For a video tutorial, watch http://bit.ly/magiccookiesvideo.

Blueberry Snack Cookies

Originally developed as a breakfast cookie, these gems became our go-to anytime snack by popular (kid) demand. I love this recipe too, because it gives me an opportunity to use up my ripe bananas and the ingredients are healthy and wholesome.

2 ripe bananas

½ cup (125 g) applesauce

½ teaspoon vanilla extract

1½ cups (120 g) old-fashioned oats

½ cup (75 g) blueberries

Preheat the oven to 350°F (180°C) and line a baking sheet with parchment paper. In a medium bowl, mash bananas with a fork. Add applesauce and vanilla and combine well. Mix in old-fashioned oats and thoroughly combine until you have a thick batter. Fold in blueberries. Scoop the batter onto lined baking sheet, 1 heaping tablespoon-size scoop at a time. Bake for 20 to 25 minutes, or until light and golden brown.

YIELD: 9 cookies

Peaches and Cream Bread

Second only to the blueberry bread from *The Best Homemade Kids' Lunches on the Planet*, this peaches and cream loaf is one that's hard to keep around! You might want to bake two—don't say I didn't warn you.

1½ cups (218 g) peaches, fresh or frozen, diced

1½ cups plus 1 tablespoon (196 g) all-purpose flour, divided

2 teaspoons baking powder

½ teaspoon salt

1 cup (230 g) plain yogurt

1 cup (200 g) sugar

3 large eggs

2 teaspoons orange zest (from 1 large orange), optional

1 teaspoon vanilla extract

½ cup (120 ml) coconut oil, in liquid form

Preheat the oven to 350°F (180°C). Grease a 9 × 5-inch (23 × 12.5 cm) loaf pan, dust with flour, and tap out excess. Alternatively, you can line loaf pan with parchment paper.

In a small bowl, mix diced peaches with 1 tablespoon flour. Use your hands to toss the peaches in the bowl until they are evenly coated with flour. This helps prevent them from sinking to the bottom of the pan when baking.

In a medium bowl, whisk together remaining flour, baking powder, and salt.

In a large bowl, or the bowl of your stand mixer, mix yogurt, sugar, eggs, orange zest (if using), vanilla, and coconut oil on low speed until all items are thoroughly combined.

Slowly add the flour mix to the wet ingredients, making sure there are no clumps but taking care not to over mix. Gently fold flour-coated peaches into the batter.

Pour the batter into the pan and bake 50 to 55 minutes, or until a toothpick inserted into the center of the loaf comes out clean.

Let bread cool in the pan for 10 minutes, and then transfer to a wire rack to cool completely before removing from pan.

YIELD: 1 loaf

Laura's Tip

If you are using frozen peaches, take them out of the freezer and transfer them onto a bowl or cutting board to thaw slightly while you measure the other ingredients. The semi-soft state will make it easier to cut the peaches into cubes.

Pear Crumble

When I'm rushing to take the kids to school and completely forget to eat breakfast, this is one of my favorite mid-morning snacks. I bake one and keep the other in the fridge for the next day or for one of the kids to snack on in the afternoon.

2 ripe pears, diced

½ teaspoon vanilla extract

2 teaspoons apple juice

1 tablespoon (15 ml) maple syrup

¼ cup (40 g) old-fashioned oats

1 tablespoon (8 g) chopped walnuts

2 teaspoons coconut oil, melted

½ teaspoon cinnamon

2 tablespoons (30 ml) heavy cream, optional

Preheat the oven to 400°F (200°C).

In a small bowl, toss diced pears, vanilla, and apple juice. Divide diced pears into two individual baking ramekins.

In a small bowl combine maple syrup, oats, walnuts, coconut oil, and cinnamon.

Top each baking ramekin with half of the crumble mixture.

Bake for 20 minutes, remove from the oven, and allow it to cool to room temperature. Top each crumble with a tablespoon (15 ml) of heavy cream (optional) and serve.

YIELD: 2 servings

Blueberry Crumble

This is a perfect way to use up leftover frozen blueberries from summer. It's great for breakfast, but it also makes a great snack or dessert!

1½ cups (220 g) blueberries, fresh or frozen

1 teaspoon lemon zest

2 teaspoons maple syrup

½ teaspoon vanilla extract

¼ cup (60 g) old-fashioned oats

1 tablespoon (8 g) chopped walnuts

1 teaspoon coconut oil, melted

Preheat the oven to 400°F (200°C).

In a medium bowl, combine blueberries and lemon zest. Divide lemon blueberries into two individual baking ramekins.

In a small bowl combine maple syrup, vanilla, oats, walnuts, and coconut oil. Top each baking ramekin with half of the crumble mixture.

Bake for 20 minutes, remove from oven, and allow it to cool to room temperature for a few minutes before serving. Top each crumble with a tablespoon (15 ml) of heavy cream (optional) and serve.

YIELD: 2 servings

Carrot Cake Muffins

While the carrot cake scones are my favorite, sometimes I just want to whip something up and let the muffin tin do all the work. Delicious, wholesome, and full of flavor, these muffins will become a breakfast and snack favorite.

2 cups (250 g) whole-wheat pastry flour or all-purpose flour

1 cup (160 g) old-fashioned oats plus 2 tablespoons (20 g) for topping, divided

2 teaspoons baking powder

½ teaspoon salt

2 teaspoons ground cinnamon

½ teaspoon ground nutmeg

½ teaspoon ground ginger

½ cup (112 g) butter, melted and cooled

2 cups (220 g) grated carrots (about 3 medium carrots)

1 cup (235 ml) milk

½ cup (170 g) honey

2 teaspoons (10 ml) vanilla extract

2 eggs, whisked

1 cup (145 g) raisins

½ cup (60 g) chopped walnuts

Preheat the oven to 375°F (190°C) and line a 12-cup muffin pan with paper liners.

In a large bowl, whisk flour, 1 cup (160 g) oats, baking powder, salt, cinnamon, nutmeg, and ginger.

In the bowl of a stand mixer, place melted butter, carrots, milk, honey, and vanilla. Mix to combine. With mixer on low speed, add eggs, mixing just enough to combine.

Slowly add the dry ingredients to the wet ingredients with the mixer on low. Mix until just combined with no dry clumps visible. Use a wooden spoon to gently fold in raisins and chopped walnuts.

Fill each muffin cup with a little over ⅓ cup (75 g) of batter. Sprinkle remaining 2 tablespoons (20 g) of oats on top.

Bake muffins for 15 to 18 minutes, or until a toothpick inserted in the center comes out clean. Remove from oven and allow muffins to cool slightly before removing from pan.

YIELD: 12 muffins

Carrot and Zucchini Bars

I have to thank my friend Michelle Castañeda for this recipe. Who knew baked veggies could taste this good?

1½ cups (195 g) carrots, shredded

1 cup (130 g) zucchini, shredded

1½ cups (187 g) all-purpose flour

1 teaspoon baking powder

¼ teaspoon baking soda

½ teaspoon cinnamon

2 eggs, beaten

¾ cup (169 g) packed brown sugar

½ cup (75 g) raisins

½ cup (120 ml) melted coconut oil

¼ cup (85 g) honey or maple syrup

1 teaspoon vanilla extract

Place shredded carrots and zucchini onto a paper towel and pat dry to absorb moisture.

Preheat the oven to 350°F (180°C).

In a large bowl combine flour, baking powder, baking soda, and cinnamon.

In another large bowl stir together eggs, carrot, zucchini, brown sugar, raisins, coconut oil, honey, and vanilla.

Add carrot mixture to flour mixture, stirring with a spatula or wooden spoon until just combined. Pour batter onto a greased 13 × 9-inch (33 × 23 cm) baking pan.

Bake for 22 to 25 min, or until a toothpick inserted into the center of the pan comes out clean. Remove from the oven and allow to cool before cutting.

YIELD: 12 servings

Oatmeal Banana Muffins

Thanks to my friend Brooke, these muffins have become the perfect busy morning breakfast staple and mid-morning school snack!

2½ cups (400 g) old-fashioned oats

1 cup (230 g) plain low-fat Greek yogurt

2 eggs

¾ cup (255 g) honey

1½ teaspoons baking powder

½ teaspoon baking soda

2 medium ripe bananas

Preheat the oven to 400°F (200°C). Line a muffin pan with paper liners.

Place oats, yogurt, eggs, honey, baking powder, baking soda, and ripe bananas in a food processor. Pulse to combine and blend until oats are smooth.

Divide batter among cupcake liners, and bake for 18 minutes, or until toothpick inserted in the center comes out clean. Remove from oven and cool to room temperature before serving.

YIELD: 12 muffins

Cherry Hand Pies

My solution to using up fruit that has been in the freezer for too long is to either make jam or make hand pies. Sometimes I make hand pies with the jam. Did I mention we love hand pies?

12 ounces (340 g) frozen cherries

⅔ cup (103 g) dried cherries

⅔ cup (133 g) sugar

1 tablespoon (8 g) cornstarch

1 tablespoon (15 ml) lemon juice

1 tablespoon (14 g) butter

2 teaspoons vanilla extract

⅛ teaspoon salt

2 layers pie dough, homemade (page 105) or store-bought

1 egg white

1 tablespoon (15 ml) water

Coarse sugar, for topping

For the icing:

1 egg white

1¼ cups (180 g) sifted powdered sugar

1 teaspoon vanilla extract

Place frozen and dried cherries, sugar, cornstarch, lemon juice, butter, vanilla extract, and salt inside a medium saucepan over medium heat. Stir frequently, until the mixture comes to a boil.

Turn heat down to a simmer and cook for 10 minutes, or until the mixture has thickened. Turn off the burner and allow the mixture to cool to room temperature, continuing to stir the mixture from time to time.

Remove the pie dough from the refrigerator and allow it to warm up for about 10 minutes so it becomes more pliable.

Preheat the oven to 400°F (200°C) and line a baking sheet with parchment paper.

Unroll piecrust, cutting it using a heart-shaped cookie cutter or any desired shape. I tend to use a 3-inch (7.5 cm) cutter.

Place a shape cut from the piecrust on a parchment-lined baking sheet, and top it with a couple tablespoons of room temperature cherry pie filling, leaving room around the edges for sealing.

Lay another heart on top, and use a fork to crimp the pie shut on all sides.

After all of the hand pies are made and sealed, place them in the refrigerator to chill for about 30 minutes.

Remove hand pies from fridge and cut a small X-shaped slit on the top of each one.

Make an egg wash by whisking together one egg white and one tablespoon (15 ml) of water. Brush each cherry hand pie with egg wash.

TO MAKE THE ICING: Beat egg white on medium-high speed until light and frothy. Add powdered sugar gradually while mixing. Add vanilla and continue mixing until fully blended.

Drizzle icing over cooled hand pies.

Bake for approximately 18 minutes, or until the crust is golden brown and the filling is bubbling through the center.

YIELD: 12 hand pies

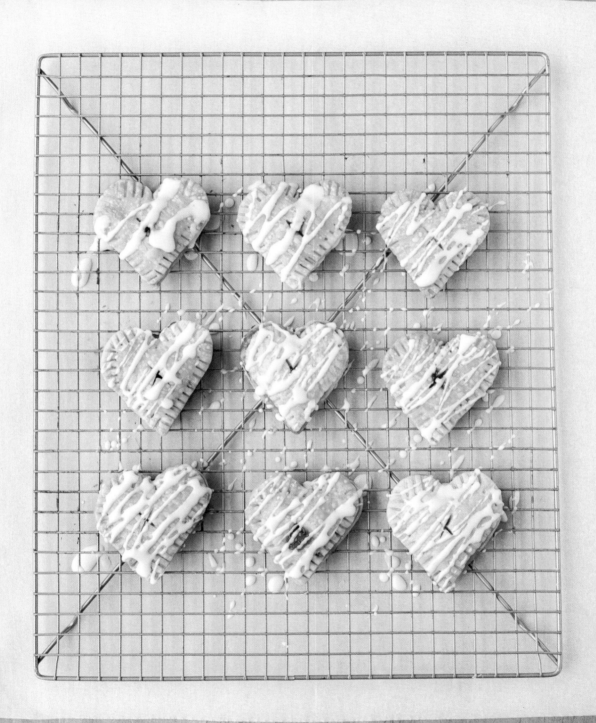

Peach Squares

These squares are my favorite. They are naturally gluten free, so it's one recipe my entire family can enjoy!

2 tablespoons (16 g) cornstarch

2 tablespoons (30 ml) warm water

2 cups (340 g) peaches, finely diced

½ cup (120 ml) maple syrup or honey, divided

1 tablespoon (13 g) sugar

2¼ cups (180 g) quick oats

1 teaspoon ground cinnamon

1 cup (260 g) peanut butter

¼ cup (61 g) pumpkin purée

1 large egg, beaten

½ cup (55 g) sliced almonds

In a small dish, whisk cornstarch and warm water until the cornstarch is dissolved and there are no more clumps. Set aside.

In a medium saucepan, combine peaches, ¼ cup (60 ml) maple syrup, and sugar. Bring mixture to a boil, cook for 3 minutes, and remove from heat.

Add cornstarch liquid and stir until it's completely dissolved into the peach mixture. Allow mixture to cool to room temperature and thicken, about 30 minutes.

Preheat the oven to 325°F (170°C). Line an 8 × 8-inch (20 × 20 cm) pan with parchment paper, leaving a 2-inch (5 cm) overhang on two sides for easy lifting.

In a large bowl, or inside a food processor, combine quick oats, cinnamon, peanut butter, remaining ¼ cup (60 ml) of maple syrup, pumpkin purée, and egg. Mix until the mixture is evenly coated. Reserve ½ cup (40 g) of the oat mixture.

Transfer remaining oat mixture to the prepared pan, pressing down to make a compact crust.

Spread peach filling on top of the oat crust. Sprinkle reserved oat mixture on top of the peach filling and top with sliced almonds.

Bake for 25 to 30 minutes, or until the tops are golden and the edges are light brown. Allow pan to cool completely. Lift parchment sides to remove bars from pan and slice into 9 squares.

YIELD: 9 servings

- -

KITCHEN NOTE

You can refrigerate these bars for up to 5 days or individually wrap and freeze for up to 2 months.

- -

Laura's Tip

Use strawberries, frozen cherries, blueberries, or even diced apples for the filing.

Soft Fig Cookies

These taste just like the classic soft cookie you can buy at the store, but they're made fresh in your kitchen, with only a handful of ingredients.

1⅓ cups (196 g) dried figs

1 tablespoon (20 g) honey

6 tablespoons (85 g) unsalted butter, softened

½ cup (100 g) sugar or brown sugar

1 large egg

1½ teaspoons vanilla extract

1 cup (137 g) all-purpose flour

½ cup (60 g) whole-wheat flour

1½ teaspoons baking powder

⅛ teaspoon salt

Place figs and honey in the bowl of a food processor and purée until smooth.

Preheat the oven to 350°F (180°C).

In the bowl of a stand mixer, cream butter and sugar until smooth. Add the egg and vanilla, mixing for another 2 minutes until it has a pastelike consistency.

In a small bowl, combine flours, baking powder, and salt.

On low speed, gradually add the flour mixture to the creamed sugar mixture to form a dough. Remove dough from the bowl, give it a quick hand knead, and divide in two.

Roll the first half of the dough between two pieces of parchment paper to form a 12 × 4-inch (30.5 × 10 cm) strip. Remove the top piece of parchment paper.

Spread half of the fig paste along the center third of the rectangle, working it nearly all the way to the top and bottom edges.

Using the bottom piece of parchment paper to assist you, lift one-third of the dough rectangle and fold it over the top of half of the fig paste. Repeat this process with the other side, gently pressing the dough along the centerline and top and bottom edges.

Repeat this process with the second half of the dough.

Cut each rectangular log into 8 to 10 pieces. Transfer cookie pieces to a baking sheet lined with parchment paper and bake 18 minutes, or until golden brown.

Allow the cookies to cool before serving. Store in an airtight container for up to 5 days. Alternatively, you can freeze unbaked cookies and make them another day.

YIELD: 18 to 20 cookies

Coconut Macaroons

My grandmother used to make these delicious treats and offer them, on occasion, with an afternoon tea.

3 large egg whites

¼ cup (50 g) sugar

½ teaspoon vanilla

¼ teaspoon kosher salt

5 cups (425 g) shredded coconut

Heat oven to 325°F (170°C) and line 2 baking sheets with parchment paper.

In the bowl of your stand mixer, whisk egg whites, sugar, vanilla, and salt until it's a frothy consistency and the sugar is mostly dissolved. Remove bowl from stand mixer and gently fold in coconut until combined.

Scoop rounded balls of the mixture onto parchment-lined baking sheets to form 16 macaroons.

Bake for 18 to 22 minutes, or until golden brown, rotating the baking sheets halfway through.

Allow macaroons to cool down completely before eating.

Store at room temperature in an airtight container for up to 5 days.

YIELD: 16 cookies

Energy Squares

These energy squares are the perfect bite-size snack for active kids. Packed with nuts and dried fruits, they are far superior to the packaged, brightly colored variety, which are often made with artificial ingredients.

1 cup (110 g) almonds, coarsely chopped

½ cup (48 g) sunflower seeds, chopped

⅓ cup (6 g) crisped brown rice cereal

¼ cup (35 g) raisins

¼ cup (36 g) dried blueberries

⅛ teaspoon sea salt

¼ teaspoon cinnamon

⅓ cup (115 g) brown rice syrup

Preheat the oven to 325°F (170°C). Line a 9 × 9-inch (23 × 23 cm) baking pan with parchment paper.

In a large mixing bowl, combine almonds, sunflower seeds, brown rice cereal, raisins, blueberries, sea salt, and cinnamon. Pour brown rice syrup over nuts and fruits, using a wooden spatula to evenly distribute the syrup throughout.

Pour mixture into baking pan. Place a second piece of parchment or waxed paper on top of mixture and press down to compact ingredients. Remove the top layer of paper.

Bake for 17 to 20 minutes, or until the bars begin to brown around the edges. Remove from oven and cool to room temperature.

Using excess parchment paper as handles, lift the bars out of the pan and place on a cutting board. Cut into 2-inch (5 cm) squares.

YIELD: 16 squares

Southern Biscuits

When I tried these biscuits for the first time at a New Orleans brunch, it was love at first bite. Your family is sure to love them topped with butter and jam or stuffed with berries.

2 cups (250 g) all-purpose flour

1 tablespoon (14 g) baking powder

½ teaspoon salt

3 tablespoons (60 g) honey

½ cup butter (112 g), diced, cold

⅔ cup (156 ml) whole milk, plus 1 tablespoon (15 ml) for brushing

Set your oven rack to the middle position and preheat the oven to 425°F (220°C).

Place flour, baking powder, and salt in a food processor. Pulse to combine. Add honey and butter pieces to the flour. Continue to pulse until the butter is broken into small clumps.

Transfer the mixture to a large bowl and make a well (or a volcano) in the center. Pour milk and mix with a fork until the dough is moist.

On a lightly floured surface, knead a few times until the dough holds together and is less sticky. Pat the dough and divide it into 8 biscuits. You can use a biscuit cutter or hand-shape them; I prefer the rustic, hand-shaped look.

Transfer all biscuits to a parchment-lined baking sheet. Brush the biscuits with a little milk and sprinkle them with a sugar (optional).

Bake biscuits for 12 to 15 minutes, or until the tops are golden brown. Remove from oven and cool before serving.

YIELD: 8 servings

Strawberry Shortcakes ▷

These delicious treats are perhaps one of my family's favorite weekend snacks, all made possible thanks to the Southern Biscuits we often have leftover from breakfast.

4 cups (680 g) strawberries

1½ cups (355 ml) heavy cream

2 tablespoons (26 g) sugar

8 Southern Biscuits (at left)

Wash, hull, and slice the strawberries.

FOR THE WHIPPED CREAM: Place heavy cream and sugar in the bowl of your stand mixer. Using the whisk attachment, whip the cream until it holds a soft peak. Cover and refrigerate whipping cream while you assemble shortcakes.

On a cutting board, use a serrated knife to slice the biscuits in half. Fill the bottom half of each biscuit with about ⅓ cup (57 g) strawberries and ¼ cup (60 ml) whipped cream. Top with other half of biscuit and serve immediately.

YIELD: 8 servings

Cinnamon Soft Pretzel Bites

My daughter loves the soft pretzels sold at the mall, so naturally, I made an easy homemade version just for her.

1 cup (235 ml) warm water
(100°F to 110°F, or 35°C to 45°C)

2¼ teaspoons active dry yeast

3 cups (375 g) bread flour, plus more for work surface

1 tablespoon (18 g) salt

2 tablespoons (30 g) brown sugar, packed

¼ cup (56 g) unsalted butter, softened

½ teaspoon vegetable oil

8 cups (2 L) water

½ cup (110 g) baking soda

½ cup (100 g) sugar

½ teaspoon cinnamon

3 tablespoons (42 g) butter, melted

Combine warm water and yeast in a bowl and let stand for ten minutes to activate yeast.

In the bowl of your stand mixer, combine flour, salt, and brown sugar. With the mixer on low, add softened butter and activated yeast. Scrape the sides a few times to combine.

Switch to the bread hook attachment and mix for about 5 minutes, dusting with a little more flour to make sure the dough doesn't stick to the walls of the bowl.

Once the dough is elastic, remove it from the mixer bowl, shape it into a ball, and transfer it to a lightly oiled bowl, turning to coat the dough ball with oil. Cover with a kitchen towel and refrigerate overnight or place in a warm spot for 2 to 3 hours.

Preheat the oven to 450°F (230°C), placing the racks in upper and lower third slots. Liberally oil 2 large baking sheets (about 17 × 12 inches [43 × 30 cm]).

Bring water and baking soda to a boil in a 5-quart (946 ml) saucepan.

Punch down dough and divide into quarters. Form each quarter into 4 balls. Roll each ball into a 12-inch (30 cm) long rope. Cut each rope into six 2-inch (5 cm) pieces.

Boil a dozen pretzel bites for 30 seconds, and then use a slotted spoon to transfer the bites onto the oiled baking sheets.

Bake pretzel bites in the oven, switching sheets between racks and rotating sheets halfway through baking, until browned, 8 to 10 minutes (watch closely toward the end of baking; bites brown quickly in last few minutes). Immediately transfer pretzel bites to wire racks to cool.

In a small bowl, mix sugar and cinnamon. Brush pretzel bites with melted butter, lightly dip into cinnamon sugar mixture and enjoy.

YIELD: 8 servings

Cinnamon Cheese Twists

My grandmother used to make these for breakfast in winter and serve them with homemade hot chocolate. It was her easy version of churros.

1 sheet frozen puff pastry

2 tablespoons (28 g) butter, melted

¼ teaspoon vanilla extract

¼ cup (50 g) sugar

¼ teaspoon cinnamon

All-purpose flour, for dusting

Allow the frozen puff pastry to thaw at room temperature until softened, about 30 minutes. Meanwhile, preheat the oven to 400°F (200°C). Line a baking sheet with parchment paper.

Combine melted butter and vanilla in a small bowl.

In another small bowl, mix sugar and cinnamon.

Unfold the thawed puff pastry sheet and place on a lightly floured work surface. Using a pastry brush, brush some of the butter mixture evenly over the dough. Sprinkle cinnamon sugar evenly over half of the butter-brushed dough. Fold the plain dough over the cinnamon-sprinkled side, pressing gently to seal. Brush the top with butter, and press gently to adhere to the sides. Turn the dough over, brush the other side with additional butter and press gently.

Cut the pastry lengthwise into 4 to 6 equal strips. Holding each strip by the ends, turn the ends a few times in opposite directions to create a twist. Place the twists, evenly spaced, on the baking sheet.

Bake for about 10 minutes, or until browned. Let cool briefly. Serve warm or at room temperature.

YIELD: 4 to 6 servings

Baked Cheese Twists

"Yum! These are fluffy, crispy, and cheesy!" noted my daughter when she tried these. I often pair these with ham, olives, and cucumber slices.

1 sheet frozen puff pastry

1 large egg

½ cup (40 g) shredded Parmesan cheese

½ cup (50 g) mozzarella cheese, grated

All-purpose flour, for dusting

Let the frozen puff pastry thaw at room temperature until softened, about 30 minutes. Meanwhile, preheat the oven to 400°F (200°C). Line a baking sheet with parchment paper.

Crack the egg into a small bowl or cup. Add 1 tablespoon (15 ml) water, and whisk until blended. In another small bowl, mix together the cheeses.

Unfold the puff pastry onto a lightly floured work surface. Using a pastry brush, brush some of the egg mixture evenly over the dough. Sprinkle half of the cheese mixture over half of the dough.

Fold the uncovered dough over the cheese and press to seal. Brush the top with the egg mixture, sprinkle with half of the remaining cheese, and press gently to adhere the sides. Turn the dough over, brush the other side with the egg mixture, sprinkle with the remaining cheese, and press gently.

Cut the pasty lengthwise into 4 to 6 equal strips. Holding each strip by the ends, turn the ends a few times in opposite directions to create a twist. Place the twists, evenly spaced, on the baking sheet.

Bake about 10 minutes or until browned. Let cool briefly. Serve warm or at room temperature.

YIELD: 4 to 6 servings

CHAPTER 5

REIMAGINED CLASSICS

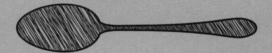

If it comes in a cute little package and has a mile-long list of (questionable) ingredients—but you or your kids still secretly love it—I've created a homemade version for you here. Say good-bye to expensive and unhealthy store-bought snacks and say hello to these even better, at-home versions!

Auntie's Perfect Pie Dough

My aunt Colleen gave me her basic pie dough recipe years ago. It's my go-to recipe for hand pies, baked goods, and snacks!

2½ cups (313 g) all-purpose flour, plus more for work surface

1 teaspoon salt

1 teaspoon sugar

1 cup (225 g) unsalted butter, chilled and cubed

4 to 6 tablespoons (60 to 90 ml) ice water

In the bowl of your food processor, combine flour, salt, and sugar. Pulse a few times to mix well.

Add cold, cubed butter to the flour mixture. Pulse together until the mixture resembles cornmeal.

Add 4 tablespoons (60 ml) ice water and pulse again until the dough forms a ball. Add 1 tablespoon (15 ml) at a time, up to two more, until the dough comes together.

Divide dough in half, flatten into a disc, and wrap with plastic wrap. Refrigerate for at least 1 hour before using.

Roll out each disc on a floured surface and follow recipe directions.

YIELD: 2 piecrusts

- -

KITCHEN NOTE

The pie dough can be made ahead of time, wrapped in plastic wrap, and kept in the fridge for up to 5 days. Or it can be made way in advance, frozen, and then placed in the fridge to defrost a couple of days before using.

- -

Chocolate-Covered Peanut Butter Cookies

My neighbor's daughter managed to sell us a few dozen Girl Scout cookies all 3 years they lived across the street. My husband's favorite cookies were the Tagalongs. Not being able to access them throughout the year forced me to get creative and make my own, and now he can enjoy them year-round.

¼ cup (65 g) creamy peanut butter

2 teaspoons (13 g) honey

⅛ teaspoon cornstarch

⅛ teaspoon vanilla extract

24 vanilla wafer cookies

1 cup (175 g) chocolate chips

In a small bowl, combine peanut butter, honey, cornstarch, and vanilla extract, stirring until well blended.

Top each vanilla wafer with approximately 1 teaspoon of the peanut butter mixture and place on a parchment-lined baking tray.

Chill cookies in the refrigerator for 1 hour.

Once cookies have been chilled, melt chocolate chips using a double boiler filled with 1 to 2 inches (2.5 to 5 cm) of water. When the chocolate is melted, turn off heat.

Coat each cookie with melted chocolate, either by dipping them individually or by gently pouring chocolate over the cookies. Place covered cookies back on the baking sheet and refrigerate until the chocolate is set, then serve.

YIELD: 24 cookies

Fresh Fruit Toaster Pastries

Why settle for dry, bland, and highly processed breakfast pastries when you can have a homemade version with fresh fruit?

For the pastries:

1½ cups (270 g) strawberries, chopped

⅓ cup (65 g) sugar

2 tablespoons (40 g) honey

2 sheets pie dough, homemade
(page 105) or store-bought

1 tablespoon (15 ml) milk

For the icing:

1 egg white

1¼ cups (180 g) sifted powdered sugar

1 teaspoon vanilla extract

Preheat the oven to 350°F (180°C) degrees and line a baking sheet with parchment paper.

TO MAKE THE PASTRIES: In a small saucepan, combine strawberries, sugar, and honey. Cook over medium heat for 25 minutes, stirring occasionally, until the strawberries have thickened. Remove from heat, transfer to a blender, and purée until smooth. Set aside to cool.

On a floured surface, roll the pie dough into a ⅛-inch (3 mm) thick rectangle. Cut the dough into 3 × 4-inch (8 × 10 cm) rectangles. Repeat with remaining dough. You will need two rectangles for each tart.

Place half of the rectangles down on baking sheet. Spoon 1½ tablespoons (23 g) strawberry filling onto the center each rectangle, making sure to spread only slightly.

With a pastry brush, brush milk along the edges of each rectangle. Lay one of the remaining rectangles of dough over the top of each. Use a fork to press down around all edges to seal. Using a sharp knife, cut a few small slits on the top of each tart, for steam to escape.

Bake tarts for about 25 to 30 minutes, or until golden brown. Remove from the oven and transfer to wire racks to cool completely.

TO MAKE THE ICING: Beat egg white on medium-high speed until light and frothy. Add powdered sugar gradually while mixing. Add vanilla and continue mixing until fully blended.

Drizzle icing over cooled tarts.

YIELD: 6 to 7 pastry tarts

Laura's Tip

Use homemade jam like the Easy Strawberry Jam, (page 56), for the cooked, fresh strawberries, sugar, and honey.

Homemade S'mores Toaster Pastries

I made these as a special treat for my son's campfire-themed class breakfast one year. They were a hit, and now we make them for special occasions.

2 layers pie dough, homemade (page 105) or store-bought

½ cup (130 g) Homemade Chocolate Hazelnut Spread (page 205)

½ cup (104 g) Marshmallow Cream Fluff (page 118)

2 tablespoons (30 ml) milk

Preheat the oven to 350°F (180°C) and line a baking sheet with parchment paper.

Fill two zip-top bags (or piping bags) with the homemade fillings—the hazelnut spread in one and the marshmallow cream in the other. Set aside.

On a floured surface, roll your pie dough into a ⅛-inch (3 mm) thick rectangle. Cut the dough into 3 × 4-inch (8 × 10 cm) rectangles. Repeat with the remaining dough. You will need two rectangles for each tart.

Place half of the rectangles down on baking sheet. Cut a small tip off the corner of each bag of filling. Pipe alternating rows of homemade hazelnut spread and marshmallow cream in the middle of each rectangle, leaving a ¼-inch (6 mm) border around the edges.

Use a pastry brush to brush milk along the edges of each rectangle. Lay one of the remaining rectangles of dough over the top of each rectangle. Use a fork to press down around all edges to seal. Using a sharp knife, cut a few small slits on top of each tart, for steam to escape.

Bake tarts for 25 to 30 minutes, or until golden brown. Remove from oven and transfer to wire racks to cool completely.

Optional: Drizzle extra hazelnut spread and lightly warmed marshmallow cream on top of the tarts to decorate.

YIELD: 6 to 8 toaster pastries

Homemade Minty Thins

Crispy, chocolatey, and delicious all in a single bite. With only 3 pantry-friendly ingredients, these are the perfect treat—and making them is a great kid-friendly food activity!

36 round whole-wheat crackers

2 cups (350 g) semisweet chocolate chips

½ teaspoon peppermint extract

Line a baking sheet with parchment paper.

Melt chocolate chips in a double boiler or in the microwave in 30-second increments, stirring frequently. Once the chocolate is melted, stir in the peppermint extract.

Using a fork, dip individual crackers into the chocolate, coating both sides. Lay coated crackers on parchment paper.

Chill in the refrigerator until the chocolate is set. Store in an airtight container for up to 1 week.

YIELD: 36 cookies

White Chocolate Raspberry Thins

My son's teacher described these bite-size treats as "luxurious and decadent-tasting." Wrap a dozen in clear bags and you have the perfect teacher's gift.

36 round whole-wheat crackers

2 cups (350 g) white chocolate chips

½ teaspoon raspberry extract

Line a baking sheet with parchment paper.

Melt chocolate chips using a double boiler or in the microwave in 30-second increments, stirring frequently. Once the chocolate is melted, remove from heat and stir in raspberry extract.

Using a fork, dip individual crackers into the chocolate, coating both sides. Lay coated crackers on parchment paper.

Chill cookies in the refrigerator until chocolate is set. Store in an airtight container for up to 1 week.

YIELD: 36 cookies

Chocolate Chia Seed Mousse

This chocolate mousse is a delicious way to take advantage of the chia seed's super nutrition with zero complaints about its "slimy" texture.

⅓ cup (55 g) chia seeds

1 cup (235 ml) milk

2 tablespoons (10 g) unsweetened cocoa powder

1 tablespoon (15 ml) maple syrup

Place all ingredients in a medium bowl or jar. Whisk well to combine, cover, and refrigerate overnight.

Just before serving, transfer pudding ingredients to your blender. Blend until smooth and serve immediately.

YIELD: 2 servings

Three-Ingredient Peanut Butter Pudding

My friend Rachel Lacy introduced me to this simple dessert. Thanks to her, we ditched all pudding mixes and those shelf-stable pudding cups.

1 banana, sliced

½ cup (130 g) peanut butter

½ cup (115 g) plain yogurt

Peanuts, for garnish (optional)

Combine the peanut butter and yogurt in a blender. Blend until smooth. Add the banana slices and blend just until smooth and no longer chunky. Refrigerate or serve immediately.

YIELD: 4 servings

Leftover-Rice Pudding

My grandmother made rice pudding a few times per month. One day, I asked her if it was her favorite dessert and she said it was her favorite way of using up leftover rice. Lucky for us, she made it a few times each month.

2 cups (475 ml) whole milk

1 cup (165 g) cooked rice

2 eggs

2 tablespoons (30 g) brown sugar

2 tablespoons (30 ml) maple syrup

1 teaspoon vanilla extract

½ teaspoon lemon zest

⅓ teaspoon cinnamon

Pinch of grated nutmeg

⅓ cup (48 g) raisins, for garnish (optional)

⅓ cup (40 g) chopped walnuts, for garnish (optional)

Preheat the oven to 350°F (180°C).

In a medium saucepan, heat the milk and rice to a slow simmer, stirring frequently so the milk doesn't burn.

In a separate large bowl, combine the eggs, sugar, maple syrup, vanilla, lemon zest, cinnamon, and nutmeg. Add the egg mixture to the milk-and-rice mixture and simmer for an additional 5 minutes, stirring occasionally. If you want to add raisins or walnuts to your rice pudding, add them in now so they soften.

Pour into an oval casserole or 8 × 8-inch (20 × 20 cm) baking dish and bake for 20 minutes. Allow rice pudding to cool to room temperature before serving.

YIELD: 4 servings

Gelatin Jigglers

This recipe is another kid favorite in my house, mainly because it's one that encourages them to play with their food!

2 cups (475 ml) grape juice, divided

3 tablespoons (21 g) plus 2 teaspoons gelatin

2 cups (475 ml) water

Pour 1 cup (237 ml) of the juice into a medium bowl. Sprinkle the gelatin evenly over the juice and let sit for 10 minutes to soften.

Pour the remaining 1 cup (237 ml) of grape juice and the water into a saucepan and bring to a simmer over medium heat. Remove from the heat, pour into the gelatin mixture, and stir to combine.

Pour the mixture into a 9 × 13-inch (23 × 33 cm) baking pan and let it cool to room temperature. Refrigerate over night or for at least 4 hours.

Once gelatin has set, dip the bottom of the pan in hot water for about 10 seconds, then invert onto a large cutting board.

Using large and small cookie cutters, cut out as many shapes as possible.

YIELD: 4 servings

Laura's Tip

Purchase gelatin in bulk and measure out what you need. Grass-fed gelatin is far superior in nutrients and can be easily purchased online.

Fruit Gummy Snacks ▶

With no artificial colors or flavorings, these are "mom approved" and my kids love them. You can also purchase chocolate-making mold trays to give these gummies fun shapes.

¾ cup (175 ml) grape juice

2 tablespoons (40 g) honey

1 cup (155 g) frozen cherries

½ cup (122 g) unsweetened applesauce

5 tablespoons (35 g) gelatin

In a small saucepan, combine grape juice, honey, and cherries and bring to a boil. Simmer for 5 to 7 minutes, stirring frequently, until cherries have softened and have begun to break apart.

Transfer mixture into a blender, add applesauce, and blend until smooth. Allow mixture to cool to room temperature.

With the blender on the lowest speed, add gelatin, 1 tablespoon (7 g) at a time until everything is thoroughly combined.

Pour mixture into an 8 × 8-inch (20 × 20 cm) pan and refrigerate for about 2 to 3 hours, or until the mixture sets.

Cut shapes with small cookie cutters or cut into rectangles using a sharp knife.

YIELD: 8 servings

Apples and Cinnamon Fruit Leather

The strawberry fruit leather in *The Best Homemade Kids' Lunches on the Planet* (Fair Winds Press, 2014) was such a huge hit with my kids, that I began experimenting with other fruit. This one is a fall favorite.

8 cups (1.2 kg) chopped apples (about 8 medium apples)

¾ cup (175 ml) apple cider

1 tablespoon (15 ml) lemon juice

1 tablespoon (20 g) honey

1 tablespoon (7 g) cinnamon

Preheat the oven to the lowest temperature setting, which will probably be somewhere in between 150°F and 200°F (65°C and 93°C). Line a rimmed baking sheet with parchment paper.

Heat apples and apple cider in a pot set over medium-low heat. Bring it to a simmer, and cover, cooking the apples for 10 to 15 minutes, until softened.

Pour cooked apples (with liquid) into a blender and process until smooth. Add lemon juice, honey, and cinnamon and pulse to combine.

Spread apple mixture onto the lined baking sheet. Don't pour too thin of a layer, or you'll have fruit crisps instead of fruit leather. If it's too thick, it will take longer to dehydrate. An even, consistent layer that isn't see-through or lumpy works best.

Bake for 4 to 6 hours, or until the fruit leather peels away easily from the parchment. Once cooled, cut into strips (along with attached parchment) and roll up. Store in an airtight container or zip-top bag.

YIELD: 12 to 14 strips, about 16 inches (40.6 cm) each

KITCHEN NOTE

All oven temperatures vary, so begin checking the fruit leather after 3½ hours of baking, and remember that the center of the tray always takes longer than the edges. If you have a dehydrator, feel free to use that instead of the oven.

Mango Fruit Leather

At certain times of the year, you can often find great deals on boxes of mangos, and when that happens, use the opportunity to make fruit roll ups!

4 cups (700 g) ripe mango, peeled and diced

2 tablespoons (30 ml) water

Place mango and water inside a blender or food processor. Purée until smooth.

Preheat the oven to the lowest temperature setting, which will probably be somewhere in between 150°F and 200°F (65°C and 93°C).

Spread an even layer of mango purée onto a parchment-lined baking sheet. Bake for 4 to 5 hours, or until the fruit leather peels away easily from the parchment. Once cooled, cut the fruit leather (with parchment) into strips, roll up and store in an airtight container or zip-top bag.

YIELD: 12 to 14 strips , about 16 inches (40.6 cm) each

- -

KITCHEN NOTE

See the fruit leather recipe on page 117 for practical tips to make this recipe a success.

- -

Marshmallow Cream Fluff

Used on occasion and definitely enjoyed in moderation, my friend Sue's simple recipe for marshmallow fluff has come in handy more than once for making a homemade version of store-bought snacks.

⅔ cup (130 g) granulated sugar

¼ cup (60 ml) room-temperature water

¾ cup (255 g) honey

3 egg whites

¼ teaspoon cream of tartar

1 teaspoon vanilla extract

Combine the sugar, water, and honey in a saucepan over medium heat and bring to a boil, stirring often. Clip on a candy thermometer and cook until the mixture reaches 246°F (120°C), continuing to stir every so often. Remove from heat and let cool slightly while you prepare your egg whites.

In the bowl of your stand mixer, beat the egg whites and cream of tartar until soft peaks form.

Add a couple of spoonfuls of the warm sugar mixture to the whipped egg whites and combine; this will slowly increase the temperature of the egg whites; do not pour in the full amount of the mixture or it will cook your eggs!

Turn the whisk attachment on low speed and slowly drizzle in the remaining mixture. Once fully incorporated, add vanilla and turn the speed to high. Beat the mixture until light and fluffy, about 10 minutes.

Use immediately or refrigerate in an airtight container for up to 2 weeks.

YIELD: Approximately 3 cups (272 g)

Marshmallow Cream—Filled Chocolate Cupcakes

When I asked my daughter's friend Elizabeth what she wanted for her birthday, she said a box of Hostess Cupcakes. Of course, you know I showed up with my own dozen.

For the cupcakes:

¾ cup (150 g) sugar

1 cup (125 g) all-purpose flour

⅓ cup (27 g) cocoa powder

1 teaspoon baking powder

1 teaspoon baking soda

½ teaspoon salt

1 egg, beaten

½ cup (120 ml) milk

½ cup (112 g) butter, melted

1 teaspoon vanilla extract

½ cup (120 ml) boiling water

1 recipe Marshmallow Cream Fluff (at left)

For the frosting:

¼ cup (44 g) bittersweet chocolate, chopped

¼ cup (60 ml) heavy cream

For the piping:

½ cup (60 g) powdered sugar

¼ cup (55 g) unsalted butter, at room temperature

1 tablespoon (15 ml) milk

¼ teaspoon vanilla extract

Preheat the oven to 350°F (180°C) and line a 12-cup muffin pan with paper liners.

TO MAKE THE CUPCAKES: In a large bowl, combine sugar, flour, cocoa powder, baking powder, baking soda, and salt.

In a separate bowl, combine egg, milk, butter, and vanilla. Add wet mixture to dry mixture. Beat for 2 minutes until everything is thoroughly combined. Add boiling water to batter (batter will be thin).

Fill muffin cups two-thirds full with batter. Bake for 22 to 25 minutes. Once cooled, remove from pan and transfer to a cooling rack.

Fill a quart-size zip-top bag with homemade fluff and refrigerate.

TO MAKE THE FROSTING: In a double boiler, melt bittersweet chocolate and heavy cream, stirring often. Turn off heat and set aside to thicken while you make the white swirl topping.

TO MAKE THE PIPING: Whisk powdered sugar, butter, milk, and vanilla until smooth. Transfer to a zip-top bag and cut off one corner to create a small opening about the size of a pencil tip.

Using a small, ½-inch (12 mm) round cookie cutter or a paring knife, cut a hole through the top of each cupcake. Fill each cupcake with homemade fluff. Then dip each filled cupcake into the chocolate ganache bowl and place on cooling rack to set.

Once the ganache is firm, take white frosting bag and pipe decorative curls across the top of each cupcake. Allow frosting to set prior to serving.

YIELD: 12 cupcakes

Homemade Tortilla Chips

After our weekly taco night, I'm always left with leftover corn tortillas. Naturally, repurposing them into baked tortilla chips to dip in my Peach Salsa (page 79) seemed like the natural thing to do.

4 corn tortillas

2 teaspoons (10 ml) vegetable oil

Salt to taste

Preheat the oven to 350°F (180°C).

Brush both sides of each tortilla with oil. Stack the tortillas on a cutting board and cut them into triangles or chip-size pieces.

Spread out in a single layer on a baking sheet and season lightly with salt.

Bake for about 12 to 15 minutes, or until golden brown and crisp, checking often to make sure the chips do not burn.

YIELD: 4 servings

Laura's Tip

Double the batch if you'd like extras—just rotate the trays halfway through baking.

Cinnamon and Sugar Baked Sweet Potato Chips

When you try these chips, you'll ask yourself where they've been all your life. These are a more nutritious and delicious alternative to store-bought potato chips.

2 sweet potatoes, peeled

3 tablespoons (42 g) butter, melted for brushing

2 tablespoons (26 g) sugar

¼ teaspoon cinnamon

Preheat the oven to 400°F (200°C). Brush two baking trays with a little melted butter.

Using a mandolin, slice sweet potatoes ⅛-inch (3 mm) thick and place them on baking trays. Lightly brush them with additional butter.

In a small bowl, combine sugar and cinnamon. Set aside.

Bake for 20 minutes, checking after 10 minutes to rotate the pans.

Once chips are done, transfer to paper towels and sprinkle with cinnamon-sugar mixture while hot.

YIELD: 4 to 6 servings

Savory Baked Sweet Potato Chips ▷

The sweet and savory versions of these chips are equally delicious. No matter which you choose, these will be the best "chips" you'll ever eat.

2 sweet potatoes, peeled

Olive oil, for brushing

Salt

Preheat the oven to 400°F (200°C). Brush two baking trays with olive oil.

Using a mandolin, slice sweet potatoes ⅛-inch (3 mm) thick and place them on baking trays. Lightly brush the slices with olive oil and sprinkle with a little salt.

Bake for 20 minutes, checking halfway through the baking time to rotate the pans. Transfer to paper towels and sprinkle with additional salt while still hot.

YIELD: 4 to 6 servings

- -

KITCHEN NOTE

Consistent potato slices are essential for even baking, and using a mandolin is the only way to achieve that.

- -

Baked Potato Chips ▷

Crispy, delicious, and super easy to make, these baked potato chips are the perfect excuse for splurging on the purchase of a mandolin. Keep it handy; after trying this recipe you'll be using it a lot.

2 medium potatoes, peeled

Olive oil, for brushing

Salt and pepper

Preheat the oven to 375°F (190°C).

Brush 2 large baking sheets lightly with oil.

Use a mandolin to cut the potatoes lengthwise into ⅛-inch (3 mm) thick slices. Arrange the slices in a flat layer on the baking sheets. Brush the slices with a thin layer of olive oil and lightly season with salt.

Bake for 15 to 20 minutes, checking at the halfway point to rotate the pans. Transfer to paper towels and sprinkle with salt and pepper while hot.

YIELD: 4 to 6 servings

Homemade Banana Chips

Next time you are at the grocery store and see overripe bananas at a special price, snatch them up! They are perfect for this recipe.

4 bananas

2 tablespoons (30 ml) lemon juice

1 tablespoon (15 ml) water

½ teaspoon cinnamon

⅛ teaspoon salt

Preheat the oven to 250°F (120° C).

Peel and slice bananas to ⅛-inch (3 mm) thickness. Place bananas on two parchment paper-lined pans.

In a small dish, mix lemon juice and water. Brush bananas with lemon water.

In a small bowl, mix together cinnamon and salt. Hold a small mesh strainer over the bananas and lightly dust all banana pieces with the cinnamon and salt mix.

Bake for 2 hours, turning all pieces at around 90 minutes.

Allow bananas to fully cool to crisp.

YIELD: 6 servings

Zucchini Chips

These taste better than the veggie chips sold at the store, and they are a whole lot healthier too!

1 medium-size zucchini

¼ teaspoon salt

1 tablespoon (15 ml) olive oil

Salt and other seasonings to taste

Using either a mandolin or a knife, slice zucchini ⅛-inch (3 mm) thick. The thinner the slices, the crispier they will become.

Lay zucchini slices on top of a few sheets of paper towels. Sprinkle the tops lightly with salt. Let slices sit for 10 minutes while the salt draws out the moisture.

Heat oven to 225°F (107°C). Line a baking sheet with parchment paper.

Blot zucchini slices dry with paper towels to remove excess moisture.

Place zucchini slices on top of the lined pan. Brush with olive oil and sprinkle with a little additional salt for seasoning, taking care not to over season.

Bake in the oven for approximately 2 hours or until the slices have reached the level of crispiness you desire.

Remove the baking sheet from the oven and allow zucchini slices to cool before serving.

YIELD: 2 servings

Baked Cinnamon Tortilla Chips

These chips are super easy to make and this is the perfect way to use up leftover tortillas from taco night.

3 tablespoons (40 g) sugar

1 teaspoon cinnamon

4 whole-grain tortillas

2 tablespoons (28 g) butter, melted

Preheat the oven to 350°F (180°C) and line a baking sheet with parchment paper.

In a small bowl, combine cinnamon and sugar; set aside.

Use a pizza cutter or knife to cut tortillas into triangles, or use cookie cutters to cut tortillas into fun shapes.

Place tortilla pieces on a baking sheet and use a basting brush to lightly coat each side with butter. Sprinkle each side with cinnamon-sugar mixture.

Bake for 10 to 15 minutes, or until lightly golden, keeping a close eye to make sure the chips do not burn. Allow tortilla chips to cool down prior to serving.

YIELD: 4 servings

Baked Apple Chips

When apples are abundant in the fall, I often bake these as a snack or lunchbox treat. Sometimes, my kids dip these chips into the Caramel Cheesecake Apple Dip (page 69).

1 cup (235 ml) apple juice

1 cup (235 ml) water

1 cinnamon stick

2 large apples

Preheat the oven to 250°F (120°C). Place a wire cooling rack inside a baking tray.

Core apples with an apple corer or a paring knife and slice as thinly as possible using either a knife or a mandolin.

Bring apple juice, water, and cinnamon stick to a boil. Place apples inside boiling liquid and cook for about 5 minutes or, until wilted and translucent.

Remove the apple chips from the pot and pat dry. Transfer to the cooling rack, place the baking tray in the oven, and bake for 40 to 50 minutes, flipping them over halfway through, until crisp and golden brown.

YIELD: 4 to 6 servings

◀ Granola Trail Mix

When I travel, I bring a big bag of this trail mix with me. It's so delicious as a snack, or mixed with fruit and yogurt for a power breakfast.

1 cup (145 g) mixed nuts

⅓ cup (60 g) white chocolate chips

⅓ cup (60 g) chocolate chips

½ cup (75 g) dried cherries

⅓ cup (25 g) large flaked coconut

1 cup (145 g) raisins

1 batch Pantry Granola (page 131)

In a large bowl, combine all ingredients. Transfer to an airtight container or zip-top bag.

YIELD: Approximately 4½ cups (450 g)

Caramel Apple Trail Mix

I love all things apple and this quick snack is one of my favorite things to create with leftover apple rings.

1 cup chopped Baked Apple Chips (page 125)

½ cup (88 g) caramel chips

1 cup (145 g) cashews

1 cup (145 g) almonds

1 cup (36 g) small pretzels

In a large bowl, combine all ingredients.

Store in an airtight container.

YIELD: 4½ cups (653 g)

Laura's Tip

If you are using store-bought apple rings, make sure you purchase the unsweetened variety. You'll find them labeled as apple rings or dried apples.

Homemade Microwave Popcorn

When I was growing up, the only way I knew how to make popcorn was with a little oil in a hot pan on the stove. While we still use that method, sometimes we just want a quick version that doesn't involve any cleanup. So when my friend Alison shared with me how easy it is to make popcorn in the microwave, my entire family was hooked. Unlike store-bought microwave popcorn, the homemade stuff does not have a scary ingredients list of artificial colors and chemicals. It is so easy to make that it may very well become a daily snack!

¼ cup (48 g) popcorn kernels

1 lunch-size brown paper bag

Salt

Pour the popcorn kernels into the bag. Fold over the top of the bag 2 or 3 times and place it folded side down in the microwave.

Press the popcorn setting on the microwave (usually around 2 minutes 30 seconds at 100 percent power). Let it run until popping slows or microwave setting is complete.

Season with salt and serve right from the bag, or poured into a bowl.

YIELD: 3 to 4 servings

Laura's Tip

Make your kids feel special by writing their names on the paper bags before microwaving.

Southern California Trail Mix ▶

In high school, my friends and I would buy frozen yogurt from a natural health food store. Their granola topping selection was impressive, and this colorful combination always made me happy. Decades later, I'm making my own, and it's even better!

1 cup (150 g) Homemade Banana Chips (page 124)

1 cup (165 g) dried mango

1 cup (170 g) dehydrated strawberries

½ cup (145 g) dried blueberries

2 cups (290 g) almonds

Mix all ingredients in a large bowl. Store in an airtight container or sealed bag for up to 1 month.

YIELD: Approximately 5½ cups (920 g)

Tropical Snowman Trail Mix

The first time my son tried coconut flakes, he asked, "What's this?" My response was, "Snowman pieces." Since then, we've renamed the tropical mix to showcase our favorite ingredient.

1 cup (80 g) unsweetened coconut flakes

1 cup (145 g) almonds

1 cup (130 g) pistachios

1½ cups (110 g) Homemade Banana Chips (page 124)

½ cup (75 g) golden raisins

½ cup (85 g) chopped dried mango

¾ cup (116 g) chopped dried pineapple

In a large bowl, combine coconut flakes, almonds, pistachios, banana chips, raisins, mango, and pineapple.

Transfer mix to a large, airtight container or sealable bag and store up to 1 month.

YIELD: Approximately 6 cups (741 g)

- -

KITCHEN NOTE
Coconut flakes are larger shavings of coconut; quite different than grated coconut.

- -

S'mores Trail Mix

One summer, our hopes for a campfire treat was dashed when it rained every day on our beach vacation. In an attempt to save the day, I created this trail mix for my kids.

2 cups (150 g) Homemade Graham Crackers (page 142), broken

½ cup (112 g) mini chocolate chips

1½ cups (220 g) salted peanuts

½ cup (66 g) mini marshmallows

Break up graham crackers into bite-size pieces.

In a medium bowl, combine graham crackers, mini chocolate chips, salted peanuts, and mini marshmallows.

Transfer to a sealable bag and store for up to 1 week.

YIELD: Approximately 3 cups (548 g)

Pantry Granola

Once you learn how to make your own granola you'll never buy store-bought again. This is a pantry staple.

For the granola:

6 cups (480 g) old-fashioned oats

1½ cups (218 g) nuts (slivered almonds, pumpkin seeds, walnuts, etc.)

1 cup (80 g) shredded sweet coconut

½ cup (85 g) whole flaxseeds

1½ cups (approximately 220 g) mix-ins
(See suggestions at right.)

½ cup (120 ml) plus 2 tablespoons (30 ml) maple syrup

½ cup (75 g) brown sugar

½ cup (120 ml) coconut oil (melted), butter, or vegetable oil

¾ teaspoon salt

Mix-in Ideas (1½ cups [180 to 220 g] total):

Raisins

Dried blueberries

Dried cherries

Dried cranberries

Dried apricots

Dates

Walnuts

Preheat the oven to 250°F (120°C).

In a large bowl, combine oats, nuts, coconut, flaxseeds, and mix-ins.

In a separate bowl, combine maple syrup, brown sugar, oil, and salt.

Combine both mixtures in larger bowl and mix well (yes, sometimes you have to use your hands here) until all is evenly coated.

Divide uncooked granola onto 2 sheet pans, spreading it evenly over the surface. Cook for 50 minutes, stirring every 15 to 20 minutes to achieve an even color.

YIELD: Approximately 8 cups (800 g)

Maple Cinnamon Roasted Chickpeas

Roasted chickpeas were one of my grandmother's favorite snacks to make for us. With the addition of a little maple and cinnamon, I'm sure this will be popular with your family as well.

1 can (15 ounces, or 425 g) chickpeas, rinsed and drained

1 teaspoon coconut oil

1 tablespoon (20 g) maple syrup

1 tablespoon (15 g) brown sugar

¼ teaspoon cinnamon

Preheat the oven to 375°F (190°C). Line a baking tray with parchment paper.

Drain chickpeas, pat dry with paper towels, and spread them on a baking tray.

Bake for 45 minutes, giving them a stir every 15 minutes to ensure that they roast evenly. Once chickpeas are crunchy, remove them from the oven. All ovens vary, so you may need to bake for an additional 5 to 10 minutes.

Meanwhile, combine coconut oil, maple syrup, brown sugar, and cinnamon in a medium bowl.

Remove chickpeas from oven and add them to the bowl of spices. Toss chickpeas until they are evenly coated.

Spread maple-coated chickpeas on the lined tray, and bake for an additional 10 minutes to caramelize.

Remove from the oven and allow chickpeas to cool to room temperature before serving.

YIELD: 4 servings

S'mores Popcorn

A big bowl of this turns our Friday movie night into a "premiere."

2 batches Homemade Microwave Popcorn (page 128)

10 Homemade Graham Crackers (page 142)

1½ cups (198 g) mini marshmallows

1¼ cups (263 g) chocolate chips, divided

Line 2 baking sheets with parchment paper and set aside.

Pop the popcorn according to recipe (page 128). Break up graham crackers into small pieces; or, if you bake a new batch for this recipe, cut them into bite-size pieces.

In a very large bowl, combine the popcorn, crackers, and mini marshmallows. Spread mixture over the two prepared baking sheets.

In a double boiler, melt chocolate chips. Immediately drizzle the melted chocolate over the popcorn, moving in a zigzag motion.

Wait 15 to 20 minutes for the chocolate to set. You can also refrigerate the trays for 10 minutes to speed up the process.

Transfer cooled popcorn back inside a large bowl or inside individual serving bowls.

YIELD: 8 servings

Homemade Caramel Corn

One day when I was watching Martha Stewart on television, she demonstrated how easy it was to make a delicious homemade version of Cracker Jack. I quickly scrambled for a piece of paper and took notes, step by step. I'm thrilled to include this recipe in a book, so I no longer have to hunt down that scrap of paper when I need it.

1 cup (225 g) corn kernels

1 tablespoon (15 ml) oil of your choice, such as coconut or canola oil

½ cup (112 g) unsalted butter

½ cup (170 g) molasses

½ cup (115 g) brown sugar, packed

1 teaspoon vanilla extract

3 cups (435 g) unsalted peanuts

14 ounces (414 ml) condensed milk

Preheat the oven to 350°F (180°C).

Pop popcorn in a large pot, ¼ cup (57 g) at a time with about 2 teaspoons of oil, making sure you add the oil and kernels to a cold pan. Or, you can follow the microwave method on page 128. As you pop the corn kernels, transfer them into a large bowl.

In a heavy saucepan, heat butter, molasses, and brown sugar, stirring often. When it boils, cook for an additional 4 minutes, taking care not to burn the mixture.

Turn down heat to a simmer and add 1 teaspoon vanilla extract. Stir in peanuts and cook an additional 2 minutes while stirring constantly. Turn off heat and add condensed milk. Stir well to combine.

Pour sweet peanut mixture over popped corn. Using two spoons, mix thoroughly, until everything is combined.

Distribute caramel coated corn over two large trays lined with parchment paper. Bake for 15 minutes, rotating the pans after 7 minutes and stirring caramel corn. Remove pans from the oven, and allow the caramel corn to cool completely. Once it's cool enough to handle, break it apart and serve.

YIELD: 24 servings

Oh-My-Goodness! Party Mix

So many fun things in one bowl—and a party pleaser too!

2 cups (60 g) toasted corn cereal, such as Corn Chex

1 cup (30 g) toasted rice cereal, such Rice Chex

1 cup (30 g) toasted wheat cereal, such as Whole Wheat Chex

1½ cups (45 g) bite-size pretzels

1 cup (145 g) mixed nuts

1 cup (260 g) creamy peanut butter

¾ cup (175 ml) maple syrup

¼ cup (55 g) salted butter, melted

1 teaspoon cinnamon

1 teaspoon vanilla extract

5 cups (40 g) Homemade Microwave Popcorn (page 128)

In a very large bowl, combine cereals, pretzels, and nuts.

In a medium saucepan over low heat, combine peanut butter, maple syrup, and butter, stirring until all ingredients are thoroughly combined and a liquid consistency. Add cinnamon and vanilla, whisking to combine.

Pour the wet ingredients over the dry mix in the bowl. Using a spatula, combine all ingredients. Spread the sticky mixture on a baking tray to cool down, taking care not to burn your hands. When the mix has cooled, add popcorn and serve.

YIELD: 8 to 9 cups (534 to 610 g)

- -

KITCHEN NOTE

If you can't find Chex cereal, substitute a total of 4 cups (120 g) of your favorite cereals.

- -

Homemade Golden Fishies

Here they are—that favorite snack packed for trips to the zoo, museum, or park. Now you can easily make your own at home. My son has claimed the master "fish cutter" title.

8 ounces (225 g), extra-sharp cheddar cheese, shredded

2 tablespoons (28 g) butter

1 cup (125 g) all-purpose flour plus more for dipping cutter

½ teaspoon baking powder

¼ teaspoon salt

¼ teaspoon onion powder

⅛ teaspoon paprika

2 tablespoons (30 ml) ice water

Place the oven rack in the center position and preheat the oven to 400°F (200°C). Line two baking sheets with parchment paper.

Place cheese, butter, flour, baking powder, salt, onion powder, and paprika in a food processor. Pulse for 30 seconds to break everything down and combine.

Continue pulsing as you add the water. Turn the food processor on for another 30 seconds until a ball forms.

Remove dough from food processor and divide into 4 balls. Wrap in plastic and refrigerate for 10 minutes.

Roll out one dough ball on a lightly floured surface. Cut out fish shapes with a mini fish-shaped cookie cutter (about ½-inch [12 mm]) and transfer the fish to a lined baking sheet.

Repeat the process with remaining dough, and bake in preheated oven for 6 to 8 minutes, or until the tops are lightly browned. Remove from the oven and allow fish to cool.

YIELD: Approximately 4 cups (960 g)

Cheese Snack Crackers

The classic cheese cracker gets a homemade, real ingredients, and no preservatives make over. I guarantee this will become a household favorite.

2 cups (240 g) grated extra-sharp cheddar cheese

¼ cup (56 g) butter, softened

1 cup (125 g) all-purpose flour, plus more for dusting

½ teaspoon salt

2 to 3 tablespoons (30 to 45 ml) milk

Preheat the oven to 375°F (190°C) and line a baking pan with parchment paper.

Place shredded cheese, butter, flour, and salt inside a food processor. Pulse, 5 seconds at a time, about 5 or 6 times, until the dough becomes coarse crumbs.

Slowly add the milk, 1 tablespoon (15 ml) at a time, with the food processor on, until the dough becomes a ball.

Divide dough into two balls and refrigerate for 15 minutes. Remove one dough ball from the refrigerator and roll it on a floured board with a rolling pin that has been floured until it is about ⅛-inch (3 mm) thick.

Cut the dough into 1-inch (2.5 cm) squares with a sharp knife or pizza cutter. You can put a bit of flour on the blade of the knife to keep it from sticking. Use a toothpick or skewer to poke a hole in the center of each cracker.

Place the crackers at least ¼-inch (6 mm) apart on parchment paper on a baking sheet. Repeat process with second ball of dough.

Bake for 12 to 15 minutes, with the rack placed in the middle of your oven, until the edges are just starting to brown. They might puff up too. If you are baking two pans at the same time, swap/rotate the pans halfway through.

Place baking sheet on a rack and let the crackers cool completely. Eat or store in a covered container up to 3 days.

YIELD: 3 to 4 cups (192 to 256 g)

KITCHEN NOTE

Store one dough ball in the fridge up to 1 week and bake. Make these gluten-free by using an all-purpose, gluten-free flour mix instead of the all-purpose flour. Look for a rice- plus starch-based mix.

Laura's Tip

Substitute other cheeses for the cheddar for a different snack every time!

Homemade Thin Wheat Crackers

Crispy, delicious, and addicting, you'll wonder why you didn't double the batch. These crackers are nearly identical to the boxed version, but made with real ingredients in your kitchen.

¾ cup (94 g) all-purpose flour

½ cup (63 g) whole-wheat flour

1½ tablespoons (20 g) sugar

½ teaspoon salt, plus extra for sprinkling

¼ teaspoon paprika

¼ cup (56 g) butter, cubed

¼ cup (60 ml) plus 2 tablespoons (30 ml) water (or more if dough is too dry)

¼ teaspoon vanilla extract

Preheat the oven to 400°F (200°C) and line two baking sheets with parchment paper.

In the bowl of a food processor, combine flours, sugar, salt, and paprika. Add cubed butter and pulse until the mixture resembles a crumbly, coarse sand.

In a measuring cup, mix together the water and vanilla. Slowly pour the liquid mixture into the flour mixture and mix well. Turn food processor on, running on dough mode, and knead until it becomes a ball. Remove dough from bowl and divide dough in half.

On a floured surface, roll out one half of the dough to 1⁄16-inch (2 mm) thick.

Using a pizza cutter, large knife, or cookie cutters, cut into whatever shape you desire. Use a spatula to place the crackers on the prepared baking sheet. Repeat with the remaining dough.

Sprinkle pieces with salt and bake for 8 to 10 minutes, watching closely, as these crackers can burn quickly.

Cool completely. Store in an airtight container for up to 5 days.

YIELD: Approximately 60 crackers

KITCHEN NOTE

Make these gluten-free by swapping out the all-purpose and whole-wheat flours with equal parts of all-purpose, gluten-free flour mix. Look for a rice- plus starch-based mix.

Laura's Tips

- Make this recipe 100 percent whole wheat by using whole-wheat pastry flour instead of all-purpose flour.

- You can freeze one half of the dough, wrapped tightly in plastic wrap and inside a zip-top bag, for up to 1 month.

Homemade Graham Crackers

This is the first recipe I sought out to remake at home after watching Alton Brown make them on TV years ago. A food scale is crucial for this recipe, so think of this as an opportunity to teach your kids a new kitchen skill.

6 ounces (170 g) graham flour

4 ounces (114 g) all-purpose flour

3 ounces (85 g) brown sugar

¾ teaspoon baking powder

½ teaspoon baking soda

½ teaspoon salt

⅛ teaspoon cinnamon

3 ounces (85 g) unsalted butter, cut into cubes

2 ounces (60 ml) molasses

3 tablespoons (45 ml) whole milk

½ teaspoon vanilla extract

Place graham flour, all-purpose flour, brown sugar, baking powder, baking soda, salt, and cinnamon in the bowl of a food processor. Pulse to combine.

Add butter cubes and pulse until the mixture resembles a coarse salt. Add molasses, milk, and vanilla and process the dough until a ball forms.

Remove dough from the food processor, wrap in plastic wrap, and refrigerate for 30 minutes.

Preheat the oven to 350°F (180°C).

Unwrap chilled dough and place it between two sheets of parchment paper. Roll out the dough to ⅛-inch (3 mm) thick. Transfer dough and parchment paper to a baking sheet. Remove the top sheet of parchment paper and use a pizza cutter or sharp knife to cut the dough into 2-inch (5 cm) square pieces. Trim off any excess, and use a toothpick to poke holes on the top of each square.

Bake in the middle rack of the oven for 22 to 25 minutes, or until the edges begin to brown. Remove from the oven and transfer the sheet of parchment paper onto a cooling rack.

Allow crackers to cool completely before completely separating them. Store in an airtight container for up to 1 week.

YIELD: 25 to 30 crackers

Refried Bean Dip

My husband, lover of the creamy refried bean and cheese side dish served at Mexican restaurants, asked me to make a homemade version for dinner. I tried, but I overcooked the beans and they were a lot more tender than I anticipated. My solution? Blend the whole thing into a dip! Instantly, it became a family favorite.

1 pound (500 g) dry pinto beans

8 cups (950 ml) water

2 tablespoons (28 g) butter

1½ teaspoons taco seasoning

½ cup (58 g) cheddar cheese, shredded, plus more for topping

½ cup (58 g) Monterey Jack cheese, shredded, plus more for topping

The day before, soak beans overnight in enough cold water to cover the beans by 3 inches (7.5 cm).

Rinse beans thoroughly and place them in a slow cooker with 8 cups (950 ml) of water. Cook on low for 8 to 10 hours, stirring a few times throughout.

Once beans are cooked, remove 2 cups (475 ml) of water from the slow cooker and drain remaining beans using a colander.

Place cooked beans, 1½ cups (355 ml) reserved water, butter, and taco seasoning inside a blender. Cover and blend on low speed for 1 minute until the texture is creamy. If it's too thick, slowly add the remaining ½ cup (120 ml) reserved water, a few tablespoons at a time, until you reach your desired consistency.

Pour creamy mixture into a large bowl, add shredded cheeses, and mix to combine.

Heat up just before serving, top with additional cheese, and serve with Homemade Tortilla Chips (page 121).

YIELD: 6 to 8 servings

Game Day Dip

My son calls this "man dip" because Dad loves to have it on game day. Paired with my Homemade Tortilla Chips, this dip is a hit!

1 tablespoon plus 1 teaspoon (20 ml) oil, divided

½ pound (200 g) lean ground beef (or turkey)

½ cup (80 g) diced onions

1 recipe Momveeta (at right)

Heat 2 teaspoons of oil in a medium pan over medium-high heat. Add ground beef (or turkey) and cook, stirring, until browned. Remove from pan and drain oil.

Heat remaining 2 teaspoons of oil in the pan and cook onions until soft and translucent, about 5 to 7 minutes. Add beef back into the pan, and heat through. Meanwhile, prepare your Momveeta Cheese recipe.

Combine beef and onions with the cheese into a small slow cooker. Keep warm on low temperature setting while serving.

YIELD: 12 servings

Momveeta Cheese

This is the holy grail of cheese block replacements. It's been downloaded more than 100,000 times from MOMables.com and performs just as well as the store-bought fake cheese block. It's the base for the Game Day Dip (at left), DIY Nachos (page 174), and a 1:1 replacement in any recipe that calls for the processed stuff.

16 ounces (240 g) natural American cheese

8 ounces (160 g) sharp cheddar cheese

1 cup (235 ml) milk

1 teaspoon ground cumin

Microwave Directions
Place all ingredients in a large microwave-safe bowl. Microwave on high for 5 minutes, stopping to stir every 1 to 2 minutes. The mixture might seem watery during the first few stirs, but should come together as a nice runny dip after all the cheese is melted.

Crockpot Directions
Place all ingredients in a small crockpot (one that will fit at least 4 cups [950 ml] of liquid, such as the 1.5-quart [1.5 L] size). Turn crockpot on low and cook for 2½ hours. Mix ingredients every hour to prevent cheese from sticking to the insert.

YIELD: Approximately 4 cups (950 g)

- -

KITCHEN NOTE

If you can't find American cheese, substitute a cheese such as Fontina or Colby, which melts perfectly in a fondue.

- -

Homemade Queso Dip

This is the best cheese dip you'll ever serve. Perfect for football games and parties, this is one dip everyone will devour.

1 recipe Momveeta Cheese (page 144)

1 can (10 ounces, or 280 g) diced tomatoes and green chilies, drained

Microwave Directions
Follow directions to create Momveeta Cheese on page 144. In the final microwave minute, add diced tomatoes and green chilies. Mix to combine and continue to heat the final minute.

Crockpot Directions
Place all ingredients in a small crockpot (that will fit at least 4 cups [950 ml] of liquid). Turn the crockpot on low for 2½ hours.

Mix ingredients every hour to prevent cheese from sticking to the sides of the insert.

YIELD: Approximately 4 cups (950 g)

Homemade BBQ Beef Jerky

My friend Monica introduced me to the world of grain-free cooking and paleo recipes. One day, she brought a piece of jerky to the office and I was sold on this being a delicious snack!

1 to 2 pounds (450 to 900 g) flank steak

⅓ cup (78 ml) barbeque sauce

Place the flank steak in the freezer for 2 hours to make it easier to slice.

Using a sharp knife, remove all visible fat from the meat and slice into ⅛-inch (3 mm) pieces.

Place beef slices and barbeque sauce in a large, resealable bag. Refrigerate for 24 hours to marinate.

Oven Method
Preheat the oven to the lowest possible setting between 150°F and 200°F (65°C and 93°C). Place two wire racks inside two baking pans.

Position marinated beef on the wire racks close together, but not so close that the pieces touch. Bake for 8 to 10 hours, depending on the thickness of the beef, flipping once halfway through.

Dehydrator Method
Place marinated beef on parchment-lined dehydrator trays so the pieces aren't touching.

Dehydrate the beef at 145°F (63°C) for 4 hours, flipping it once halfway through.

YIELD: 8 to 12 servings

- -

KITCHEN NOTE

If you have a convection oven setting, baking time might be 2 to 3 minutes faster.

- -

CHAPTER 6

MINI MEALS

Some days you need portable snacks to feed hungry kids on the go. The mini meals in this section are perfect for those of us who want to avoid the unhealthy fast-food drive-through and last minute snack scramble. These recipes are not quite big enough to be considered a meal but provide more sustenance than the usual four-bite snack.

Avocado Egg Salad Wraps

If you are looking for a protein-rich snack or mini meal, this is it! This recipe comes together quickly with perfectly hard-boiled eggs!

4 hard-boiled eggs, peeled and diced

1 large avocado, cubed

2 tablespoons (28 g) mayonnaise

½ teaspoon cumin powder

¼ teaspoon salt

4 whole-wheat tortillas

Place eggs, avocado, mayonnaise, cumin, and salt in a large bowl. Using a fork, mash ingredients to combine.

Lay tortillas on a flat surface. Divide Avocado Egg Salad mixture evenly on the center of each wrap.

Roll tightly and cut wraps in half before serving.

YIELD: 4 servings

Easy-to-Peel Hard Boiled Eggs

Hard boiled eggs make great snacks on their own or in other recipes. Having them handy is always a relief when I'm searching the fridge for a quick serving of protein. My method yields perfect eggs every time.

12 large eggs

1 tablespoon (18 g) salt

Water

Place eggs in a large pot and cover with at least 2 inches (5 cm) of cold water. Add salt.

Over high heat, bring the water to a boil.

When water reaches a rolling boil, turn off heat, and cover. Let eggs sit in the water for 13 minutes.

After exactly 13 minutes, carefully remove eggs from the pot and place them in a large bowl filled with iced water. Allow eggs to cool for 5 to 10 minutes.

Carefully crack each eggshell in several places, making sure most of the shell is cracked. Gently begin removing the shell. Dip the egg, as needed, into the iced water to help remove remaining shell.

YIELD: 12 servings

Laura's Tips

- Make hard-boiled eggs once a week and store in the fridge for up to 5 days for a quick, grab-and-go snack!
- Watch the video: http://bit.ly/hardboiledegg.

Classic Deviled Eggs

This is a basic recipe I use often at my house. The smoked paprika is my grandmother's doing, and I think of her every time I make these eggs.

6 Easy-to-Peel Hard Boiled Eggs (page 149)

¼ cup (60 g) mayonnaise

1 teaspoon Dijon mustard

⅛ teaspoon smoked paprika

Salt and pepper, to taste

After cooling, cut eggs in half lengthwise, carefully remove yolks, and place them in a small bowl.

Mash egg yolks with a fork. Add mayonnaise, mustard, and smoked paprika and stir with the fork until smooth. Season with a little salt and pepper and mix.

Fill a medium zip-top bag with yolk mixture, cut the tip off a corner of the bag, and pipe mixture into egg white cavity. Sprinkle with a little additional paprika.

YIELD: 6 servings

Greek Deviled Eggs

My dad can make some pretty delicious stuff with his hummus I tell you, and this is one of those recipes. The hummus adds a little extra protein and fiber to this great snack.

6 Easy-to-Peel Hard Boiled Eggs (page 149)

¼ cup (60 g) Homemade Hummus (page 74)

2 tablespoons (15 g) pitted Kalamata olives, finely chopped

⅛ teaspoon smoked paprika

Salt and pepper, to taste

After cooling, cut eggs in half lengthwise, carefully remove yolks, and place them in a small bowl.

Mash egg yolks with a fork. Add hummus, chopped olives, and smoked paprika and stir with the fork until smooth. Season with a little salt and pepper and mix.

Fill a medium zip-top bag with yolk mixture, cut the tip off, and pipe into egg white cavity. Sprinkle with additional chopped Kalamata olives.

YIELD: 6 servings

Laura's Tip

Substitute plain Greek yogurt for the mayonnaise. The eggs are just as delicious and more nutritious!

Avocado Deviled Eggs

I love using avocados to obtain a creamy filling for these deviled eggs. I try to sneak them in as much as I can, since they are rich in vitamin K, vitamin B9, vitamin B5, vitamin C, and vitamin E. The bonus is that they also add fiber! If you are a parent, you know that every little bit helps!

6 Easy-to-Peel Hard Boiled Eggs (page 149)

⅓ cup (75 g) mashed avocado (about ½ large avocado)

¼ teaspoon cumin

Salt and pepper, to taste

After cooling, cut eggs in half lengthwise, carefully remove yolks, and place them in a small bowl.

Mash egg yolks with a fork. Add avocado and cumin and stir with the fork until smooth. Season with a little salt and pepper and mix.

Fill a medium zip-top bag with yolk mixture, cut the tip off a corner of the bag and pipe yoke filling into egg white cavity.

YIELD: 6 servings

Pesto Deviled Eggs

When my daughter didn't want to eat hard-boiled eggs, I played around with the flavorings. The pesto deviled eggs were her favorite, since they reminded her of her favorite Italian meals.

6 Easy-to-Peel Hard Boiled Eggs (page 149)

¼ cup (60 g) mayonnaise

2 tablespoons (30 g) Homemade Pesto (page 76)

Salt and pepper, to taste

After cooling, cut eggs in half lengthwise, carefully remove yolks, and place them in a small bowl.

Mash egg yolks with a fork. Add mayonnaise and pesto and stir with the fork until smooth. Season with a little salt and pepper and mix.

Fill a medium zip-top bag with yolk mixture, cut a tip off the corner of the bag, and pipe yoke filling into egg white cavity.

YIELD: 6 servings

Pesto Tortilla Pinwheels

In the summer, when basil is abundant, I make a lot of pesto. These pesto pinwheels are just another way of having a little taste of summer all year long.

8 ounces (225 g) cream cheese, softened

½ cup (130 g) Homemade Pesto (page 76)

⅔ cup (53 g) shredded Parmesan cheese

4 large whole-grain tortillas or wraps

½ pound (225 g) thinly sliced turkey or ham, optional

In a bowl, or food processor, combine cream cheese, pesto, and Parmesan cheese until smooth.

Spread ¼ of the mixture on one side of each tortilla. If desired, top with 2 thin slices of roasted turkey, enough to cover the middle of the tortilla leaving a 1-inch (2.5 cm) rim.

Roll up tortilla tightly and wrap with plastic wrap. Refrigerate 2 hours.

Remove from refrigerator and unwrap. Slice into rounds and serve on a plate or tray.

YIELD: 4 to 6 servings

- -

KITCHEN NOTE

Wrapping and refrigeration isn't required but it makes it easier to slice the tortillas evenly. I often prep these the night before and have them in the fridge ready for a snack on the go.

- -

Peanut Butter Apple Wraps

Who knew you could mix fruit and veggies and make it taste this good? I think the secret ingredient may be the peanut butter, which adds a punch of protein and goes with just about anything.

½ cup (130 g) creamy peanut butter

4 whole-wheat or spinach tortillas

¾ cup (90 g) finely chopped apple

⅓ cup (37 g) shredded carrot

⅓ cup (50 g) Pantry Granola (page 131)

1 tablespoon (7 g) ground flax

Spread 2 tablespoons (32 g) peanut butter on one side of each tortilla.

Sprinkle apple, carrot, granola and flax evenly over each tortilla. Roll up tightly, cut in half, and serve.

YIELD: 4 to 8 servings

Laura's Tip

Make these wraps gluten free by using gluten-free tortillas.

Elvis Rice Cakes

I'm pretty sure if Elvis had to go gluten-free or low-carb, he'd turn his favorite sandwich into a rice cake treat!

4 slices bacon

⅓ cup (87 g) crunchy peanut butter

4 whole grain rice cakes

1 banana, sliced

½ teaspoon cinnamon

Cook bacon to a crispy texture and chop into small pieces. Set aside.

Spread 1½ tablespoons (24 g) crunchy peanut butter onto each rice cake. Sprinkle bacon over peanut butter, top with banana slices, and dust cinnamon over the bananas.

YIELD: 4 servings

Strawberries and Cream Rice Cakes

Rice cakes don't have to be a boring snack. This recipe is sweet, delicious, and full of crunch!

3 tablespoons (45 g) whipped cream cheese

2 whole-grain rice cakes

⅔ cup (113 g) strawberries, sliced

Spread 1½ tablespoons (22 g) cream cheese onto one side of each rice cake. Top with strawberry slices.

YIELD: 2 servings

Lox Rice Cakes

This delicious snack is inspired by the traditional bagel combination, only it's better for you. Add capers and thinly sliced red onion if desired.

3 tablespoons (45 g) whipped cream cheese

2 whole-grain rice cakes

4 ounces (115 g) smoked salmon

1 teaspoon lemon juice

Spread 1½ tablespoons (22 g) cream cheese onto one side of each rice cake. Top with smoked salmon slices.

Squeeze lemon juice over salmon and serve.

YIELD: 2 servings

Peanut Butter Cup Rice Cakes

This is the ultimate rice cake for peanut butter lovers. With the crunchy rice, creamy peanut butter, and rich chocolate, this almost qualifies as a candy bar.

3 tablespoons (48 g) peanut butter

2 whole-grain rice cakes

1 tablespoon (16 g) Homemade Chocolate Hazelnut Spread (page 205)

Spread 1½ tablespoons (24 g) peanut butter onto one side of each rice cake.

Spread half of the chocolate hazelnut spread onto each peanut butter-topped rice cake, swirling both spreads together to combine flavors.

YIELD: 2 servings

Cinnamon–Raisin Rice Cakes

A snack after my own heart: Cinnamon raisin is the ultimate comfort combination, don't you think?

3 tablespoons (48 g) almond butter

2 whole-grain rice cakes

Dash cinnamon

1 tablespoon (9 g) raisins

Spread 1½ tablespoons (24 g) almond butter onto one side of each rice cake.

Sprinkle a dash of cinnamon onto each rice cake and top with raisins.

YIELD: 2 servings

Mini Cuban Sandwiches

These tasty snacks are a bite-size version of one of my daughter's favorite sandwiches. I often let the kids assemble the "towers" and I take care of the broiling.

3 tablespoons (42 g) mayonnaise

1 tablespoon (11 g) Dijon mustard

40 round whole-grain crackers

10 thin slices ham

5 thin slices baby Swiss cheese, cut into quarters

20 kosher dill pickle slices

Preheat the oven broiler on low and position oven rack 6 inches (15 cm) from the top. Line a large baking sheet with parchment paper.

In a small bowl, combine mayonnaise and Dijon mustard. Spread a thin layer of the mixture onto the flat side of every cracker.

Place 20 crackers, mustard side up, on the prepared baking sheet. Top with half a slice of ham, folded. Then top ham with quartered slices of cheese.

Place the baking sheet under the broiler until cheese is melted and bubbly, about 2 minutes. Remove from oven.

Top each mini bite with one pickle slice. Top pickles with remaining crackers, mustard side down. Serve immediately.

YIELD: 20 mini sandwiches

Kid Crunchy Rolls

When I first made these rolls for my family, my son Alex, who was 5 at the time exclaimed, "These should be served everywhere, mom!" I couldn't have asked for a better review.

½ cup (112 g) almond butter

3 tablespoons (45 g) cream cheese

1 tablespoon (20 g) honey

¼ cup (36 g) raisins, chopped

6 slices soft whole-grain bread, crusts removed

⅓ cup (12 g) cornflake cereal

In a small bowl, mix together almond butter, cream cheese, and honey until it becomes a cohesive creamy mixture.

Toss in chopped raisins and fold to combine.

On a flat surface, roll each bread slice with a rolling pin to flatten. Spread 2 tablespoons (40 g) of creamy mixture onto one side of each slice. Sprinkle each slice with 1 tablespoon (2 g) of corn cereal.

Roll up each slice as tightly as possible, taking care to not rip the bread. Cut each roll into ½-inch (1 cm) thick slices with a serrated knife and serve.

YIELD: 6 servings

Pizza Poppers

"Look mom! A whole pizza bite fits in my mouth." Boys will be boys, so you might want to make sure yours take at least one bite each time.

¾ cup (94 g) all-purpose flour

¾ teaspoon baking powder

1 tablespoon (6 g) Italian seasoning

Pinch of salt

Pinch of red pepper flakes (optional)

1 egg, lightly beaten

¾ cup (176 ml) whole milk

1 cup (115 g) shredded mozzarella cheese

¼ cup (25 g) grated Parmesan cheese

1 cup (110 g) chopped pepperoni slices

½ cup (120 ml) pizza sauce

Preheat the oven to 375°F (190°C). Grease a 24-cup mini muffin pan.

In a large bowl, whisk together flour, baking powder, Italian seasoning, salt, and red pepper flakes, if using.

Whisk in the egg and milk. Stir in the mozzarella, Parmesan, and pepperoni until mixture is combined. Let mixture sit for 10 minutes. Divide mixture equally among the mini muffin cups.

Bake 20 to 25 minutes, or until the tops are puffy and golden. Remove from the oven.

Heat pizza sauce in the microwave or on the stove and serve alongside pizza poppers.

YIELD: 6 servings

Honey Wheat Biscuits

I nearly always double our favorite breakfast recipe and save extras for quick mini sandwiches for snack time. Do not attempt to make this recipe with 100 percent whole-wheat flour or the biscuits will be very dense.

1 cup (125 g) all-purpose flour, plus more for dusting

1 cup (120 g) whole-wheat flour

¼ teaspoon salt

1½ tablespoons (7 g) baking powder

6 tablespoons (85 g) very cold unsalted butter

¾ cup (175 ml) milk plus additional for brushing

2 tablespoons (40 g) honey, optional

Preheat the oven to 425°F (220°C).

In the bowl of your stand mixer or in another large mixing bowl, combine the flours, salt, and baking powder. Stir together.

Using a cheese grater, shred the butter and add it to the bowl. I always store a few sticks of butter in the freezer for this very purpose, as the colder the butter is, the better. Using your hands, mix the butter into the flour mixture until it's crumbly and evenly combined.

Form a well in the middle of the dry ingredients and add the milk and honey, if using. Stir the flour mixture into the milk until a dough forms. Don't overmix.

Sprinkle some flour on your counter, remove the dough from the bowl, and hand-knead it on the counter. Add additional flour as needed, until the dough is no longer sticky. Roll dough with a rolling pin to about an inch (2.5 cm) thick. Cut the dough with 2-inch (5 cm) biscuit cutter (or the top of a large glass). After the fourth biscuit you might need to reshape and roll the dough to cut the final two biscuits.

Line a baking sheet with parchment paper or a silicone mat. Evenly space the six biscuits on the baking sheet. Brush the tops with milk and bake for 13 to 15 minutes, or until the biscuits are a light golden brown.

YIELD: 6 large biscuits

- -

KITCHEN NOTE

You must use a cheese grater for the butter. When I tested this recipe by cutting the butter into very small pieces with a knife, the dough did not rise well and the biscuits had dense spots. So trust me; it's worth the 20 seconds it will take to grate the very cold butter.

- -

Favorite Friday Night Pizza

Here's my recipe for our Friday movie night. The dough is also the base for many other filling snacks.

For the dough:

1 cup (235 ml) plus 2 tablespoons (30 ml) warm water (120°F, 250°C)

1 tablespoon (12 g) active dry yeast

1 tablespoon (20 g) honey

1 tablespoon (15 ml) olive oil

3 cups (375 g) all-purpose flour, plus more for dusting

1 teaspoon salt

For the pizzas:

½ to 1 cup (120 ml to 235 ml) pizza sauce

½ cup (60 g) mozzarella cheese, shredded

Toppings of your choice, such as sliced onions, green peppers, olives, sliced mushrooms, pepperoni, or cooked sausage

TO MAKE THE DOUGH: In a small bowl, combine warm water, yeast, honey, and olive oil. Mix with a spoon and let the mixture rest about 10 minutes, allowing time to activate the yeast. Once you see 1 to 2 inches (2.5 to 5 cm) of "froth," the yeast is done.

In the bowl of your stand mixer or in another large mixing bowl, add the flour and salt. Mix well. Slowly add the frothy water, and mix it (either with your hands or with the paddle attachment) until you can form a dough ball.

Dust the countertop with flour. Place the dough on the countertop and give it a thorough, quick knead. You might need to add a little more flour to finish off the dough. The dough shouldn't be super sticky or rock hard. Good pizza dough should have the consistency of brand-new Play-Doh or softer.

Rub the same bowl with olive oil then place the dough inside, giving it a turn or two to coat with oil. Cover with a towel, and place it in a warm place to rise for 1 to 1½ hours.

After dough has risen, transfer it to a floured surface, and knead it a couple of times.

Oil a baking sheet and spread the dough on the sheet with lightly oiled hands to make one large rectangular crust. Or divide the dough into two even portions, and make two smaller crusts.

TO MAKE THE PIZZAS: Preheat the oven to 375°F (190°C). Top pizza dough with sauce, toppings, and cheese. Bake for about 25 minutes, or until the cheese is bubbly and the crust is golden.

YIELD: 2 medium-size pizzas or 1 extra-large pizza

Laura's Tip

For a nice, crisp outer crust, I like to use my pizza stone in a high-heat oven for a shorter cooking time. I bake this at 500°F (250°C) for 10 to 12 minutes. You can, of course, use your stone at 375°F (190°C) for 25 minutes.

Biscuit Pizzas

One day, when I didn't have English muffins around, I used our leftover biscuits from breakfast to make these pizzas. It was an instant success with the kids (and adults), and we added this new favorite to our growing list of go-to snacks.

6 Honey Wheat Biscuits (page 160), halved

1 cup (235 ml) pizza sauce

1¼ cups (150 g) shredded mozzarella cheese

Toppings of choice

Preheat the oven to 400°F (200°C). Line a baking pan with parchment paper.

Spread 1 to 2 tablespoons (15 to 30 ml) pizza sauce on each biscuit half. Add your favorite toppings, sprinkle with cheese, and place pizzas on the baking pan.

Bake for 10 to 12 minutes, or until the cheese is melted and the crust is heated through.

YIELD: 6 servings

English Muffin Pizzas ▶

I'm not sure if it's the smaller size of these pizzas or the fact that kids can easily assemble them on their own, but this snack is a hands-down favorite among kids.

6 English muffins, split and toasted

1 cup (235 ml) pizza sauce

1¼ cups (150 g) shredded mozzarella cheese

Toppings of choice

Preheat the oven to 400°F (200°C). Line a baking pan with parchment paper.

Spread 1 to 2 tablespoons (15 to 30 ml) pizza sauce on each muffin half. Sprinkle with cheese, add toppings, and place on baking pan.

Bake for 10 to 12 minutes, or until the cheese is melted and the crust is heated through.

YIELD: 6 servings

Laura's Tip

I like to line up bowls filled with the toppings on the counter and let the kids create their own mini pizzas. Try green peppers, mushrooms, nitrate-free pepperoni, ham, and black or green olives.

Berry Chocolatey Pizza

My kids have never turned down pizza or chocolate, so I figured I'd try my favorite dough with the best of both worlds. This is now a birthday party favorite!

1 homemade pizza dough recipe, (page 161)

⅔ cup (170 g) Homemade Chocolate Hazelnut Spread (page 205)

¾ cup (130 g) mini white chocolate chips

1½ to 2 cups (220 to 340 g) mixed berries

Prepare pizza dough according to directions on page 161.

Divide dough into two even balls. On a floured surface, roll out each pizza dough to desired thickness; I like mine about ¼-inch (6 mm) thick.

Preheat the oven to 375°F (190°C) and line two baking sheets with parchment paper. Position oven racks in the middle position and one shelf lower.

Transfer pizza dough onto the parchment-lined baking sheets and place in the oven for 10 minutes to begin cooking dough.

Remove the pizza crusts from the oven and spread half of the chocolate hazelnut spread over each pizza base, top with half of the berries, and sprinkle with white shredded chocolate chips.

Bake each pizza for an additional 12 to 15 minutes making sure you switch tray positions.

YIELD: 8 to 12 servings

KITCHEN NOTE

If you can't find mini chocolate chips, pulse regular-size ones in a food processor, enough to break the chips into the consistency of grated cheese.

Savory Tomato Biscuitwiches

Here is another of my favorite ways to use up leftover breakfast biscuits. Not only do these tasty bites make a great after-school snack, they'd be delicious served open-faced as an appetizer at a party as well.

4 Honey Wheat Biscuits (page 160)

¼ cup (60 g) Savory Herb-Flavored Cream Cheese (page 73)

1 large beefsteak tomato, sliced into 4 thick slices

Slice biscuits in half and lightly toast in your toaster or toaster oven.

Spread a half tablespoon (7 g) of Savory Herb-Flavored Cream Cheese onto each biscuit half. Place a thick slice of fresh tomato onto one biscuit half and top with the other biscuit half. Enjoy immediately.

YIELD: 4 biscuit sandwiches

Bacon-Wrapped Potatoes

When you have hungry teenagers who want "man food" for a snack, whip up a batch of these bacon-wrapped potatoes.

12 small red potatoes, washed

1 teaspoon salt

1 tablespoon (15 ml) olive oil

¼ teaspoon freshly ground pepper

12 slices thick-cut bacon

Preheat the oven to 400°F (200°C). Cut potatoes in half.

Place potatoes inside a large pot, cover with water, season with salt, and bring to a boil. Add potatoes and cook potatoes for 5 minutes. Drain the potatoes and transfer them to a large bowl.

Toss the potatoes with olive oil and freshly ground pepper, mixing until they are thoroughly coated.

Cut the bacon slices in half. Wrap each potato half with a half bacon slice, and secure with a toothpick. Place the potatoes on a parchment-lined baking sheet.

Bake for 15 minutes, flip, and cook for another 15 minutes. Watch potatoes and bacon very closely after the second 10 minutes. Cooking time will vary by oven and depending on the size of your potatoes.

Remove from oven and serve.

YIELD: 24 bites

Fluffy Pigs ▶

My grandmother always kept a box of puff pastry in her freezer for the occasional "merienda." A merienda was when I had friends over after school until an hour before dinner. Never short on ideas, she would make this snack, which she called "fluffy pigs."

All-purpose flour, for work surface

1 package (17 ounces, or 490 g) puff pastry

20 all-beef hot dogs, halved

1 large egg, beaten with 1 tablespoon (15 ml) water

Ketchup and mustard for serving

Roll out puff pastry on a lightly floured work surface. Cut it lengthwise into strips ½-inch (3 mm) wide (you should be able to get 20 strips from one sheet). Roll out second sheet of puff pastry and repeat the process.

Line two baking sheets with parchment paper.

Place one hotdog half at the end of a puff pastry strip. Roll and wrap hot dog with the puff pastry strip; brushing it with the egg and water mixture to adhere the end strip. Transfer the wrapped hot dog onto the baking sheet and repeat process with remaining pieces.

Brush the tops of the wrapped hotdogs with remaining egg mixture and refrigerate for 10 to 15 minutes. Meanwhile, preheat the oven to 400°F (200°C).

Bake for approximately 22 minutes, rotating the baking trays halfway through. Piggies are done when they are puffed and golden.

Allow piggies to cool and serve with ketchup and mustard.

YIELD: 40 piggies

Pizza Breadsticks

In my experience, kids love any snack that involves dipping, so these pizza breadsticks are a winner

1 batch homemade pizza dough, page 161

¼ cup (55 g) butter, melted

¼ teaspoon garlic powder

1½ cups (175 g) shredded mozzarella cheese

⅛ cup (12 g) grated Parmesan cheese

Pizza sauce, for dipping

Preheat the oven to 375°F (190°C). Line a baking sheet with parchment paper.

Divide pizza dough into two balls. On a floured surface, roll out each ball into a 10-inch (25.5 cm) square. Transfer each square onto a piece of parchment paper.

In a small dish, combine butter and garlic powder. Brush pizza dough with garlic butter.

In a medium bowl, combine mozzarella and Parmesan cheese. Sprinkle cheese mixture onto buttered dough.

Use a pizza cutter to cut the dough into 1-inch (2.5 cm) wide strips. Transfer each parchment paper sheet onto a baking sheet.

Bake, one pan at a time, for 20 to 22 minutes, or until the dough is golden brown around edges.

Separate breadsticks with the pizza slicer and serve with pizza sauce for dipping.

YIELD: 20 servings

- -

KITCHEN NOTE

If you don't plan on making both dough balls, you can half the homemade pizza dough recipe or freeze half for another time.

- -

Pizza Bagels

I saw a variation of these in the freezer section at the grocery store and list of ingredients left me on the floor. My version is more nutritious, and you can customize the toppings to fit your kids' preferences!

6 mini bagels, split and toasted

⅓ cup (78 ml) pizza sauce

1 cup (115 g) shredded mozzarella cheese

Toppings of choice, including green peppers, mushrooms, nitrate-free pepperoni, ham, and black or green olives

Preheat the oven to 400°F (200°C). Line a baking pan with parchment paper.

Spread 1 tablespoon (15 ml) pizza sauce on each muffin half. Add toppings, sprinkle with cheese, and place on the baking pan.

Bake for 10 to 12 minutes, or until the cheese is melted and the bagel is heated through.

YIELD: 6 servings

Mini Fruit Bagel Pizzas

Truth be told, I came up with this easy recipe because sometimes calling it a pizza is a lot easier than getting my kids to eat fruit.

8 whole-grain mini bagels

½ cup (115 g) Blueberry Lemon–Flavored Cream Cheese (page 72)

2 kiwis, peeled and sliced

1 cup (170 g) strawberries, sliced

Using a serrated knife, split bagels in half. Toast bagels to a light golden color.

Spread ½ tablespoon (7 g) of Blueberry Lemon–Flavored Cream Cheese onto each bagel.

Top with a kiwi slice and a couple of strawberry slices. Serve immediately.

YIELD: 8 servings

Basic Crêpes

My grandmother made crêpes for all occasions. Her filling varied based on whatever fresh fruit was in season. These crêpes are the perfect vessel to get our kids to eat more fruit and veggies when combined with other delicious fillings.

1 cup (235 ml) milk

3 large eggs

1 teaspoon vanilla extract

1 tablespoon (20 g) honey

1 cup (125 g) whole-wheat pastry flour

¼ teaspoon salt

Pinch of cinnamon

Butter, for the pan

In a blender, combine milk, eggs, vanilla, and honey. Add the flour, salt, and cinnamon. Put the lid on and blend for 30 seconds, or until everything is incorporated, stopping to scrape down the sides as necessary.

Warm a large pan or griddle over medium heat. Coat the pan with a film of butter or nonstick cooking spray, reduce the heat to low, and pour ¼ cup (60 ml) of batter onto pan. Quickly, lift the pan and swirl it around to distribute the batter in a thin circle. If using a griddle, use the flat side of a spatula to distribute batter into a thin circle.

Cook over low heat for 1 to 2 minutes, or until the bottom begins to brown and the thin pancake is easy to lift. Gently fold the crêpe in half, and fill with your desired toppings. Fold over in thirds to close. Repeat with remaining batter.

YIELD: 8 crêpes

Awesome Banana Crêpes

I'm pretty sure my youngest son would eat these delicious crêpes every day if I'd let him. He often sits on the corner of my counter, against the wall, sneaking banana pieces while he licks the almond butter off the spoon.

1 recipe Basic Crêpes, at left

½ cup (130 g) almond butter

4 bananas, sliced

2 tablespoons (32 g) Homemade Chocolate Hazelnut Spread, page 205

Make crêpes according to recipe directions at left.

Warm the almond butter in the microwave for 10 to 15 seconds, or just long enough to make it spreadable.

Return a single crêpe to warm pan and place over low heat. Spread 1 tablespoon (16 g) almond butter over crêpe, top with sliced bananas, and drizzle with a little chocolate hazelnut spread. Fold over to close and serve. Repeat with remaining crêpes.

YIELD: 8 servings

- -

KITCHEN NOTE

Whole-wheat pastry flour is the same thing as white whole-wheat flour. However, it's different than regular whole-wheat flour. You can also use all-purpose flour for the Basic Crêpes batter, or make them gluten free by using an all-purpose gluten-free baking mix plus 1 additional teaspoon of milk.

- -

Mediterranean Crêpes

All of my favorite flavors find a place inside this nutritious crêpe!

1 recipe Basic Crêpes, page 171

1 cup (216 g) Homemade Hummus, page 74

½ cup (75 g) feta cheese, crumbled

½ cup (50 g) Kalamata olives, chopped

Make crêpes according to recipe directions, page 171.

Return a single crêpe to a pan and warm over low heat. Spread about 2 tablespoons (27 g) hummus onto the crêpe. Top with feta cheese and Kalamata olives.

Once feta cheese has softened, fold over the crêpe and close it to serve. Repeat with remaining crêpes.

YIELD: 8 servings

Apple and Cheddar Crêpes

Alison's son Samuel loves the combination of apples and cheddar. When she has extra crêpes leftover from breakfast, she often makes him these.

1 recipe Basic Crêpes, page 171

2 cups (230 g) shredded cheddar cheese,

2 apples, cored and thinly sliced

Make crêpes according to recipe directions, page 171.

Return a single crêpe to a pan and warm over low heat. Sprinkle ¼ cup (30 g) cheese onto the crêpe.

Top with a few apple slices and wait for cheese to melt. Fold over to close crêpe and serve. Repeat with remaining crêpes.

YIELD: 8 servings

Broccoli and Cheese Crêpes

I never miss an opportunity to sneak in a few extra veggies.

1 recipe Basic Crêpes, page 171

1½ cups (234 g) broccoli florets, chopped

1½ cups (180 g) shredded white cheddar cheese

Make crêpes according to recipe directions on page 171.

Return a single crêpe to a pan and warm over low heat. Sprinkle about 3 tablespoons (19 g) chopped broccoli and 3 tablespoons (15 g) cheese onto the crêpe.

Once the cheese has begun to melt, fold over the crêpe and close it to serve. Repeat with remaining crêpes.

YIELD: 8 servings

Blueberry Quesadilla

Sometimes when I don't have time to make homemade crêpes from scratch and my kids want a quick snack, I make them fruity quesadillas. These are quick, easy, and delicious!

1 whole-grain tortilla

2 tablespoons (30 g) cream cheese

⅓ cup (50 g) blueberries

On a flat surface, spread cream cheese onto the tortilla, place blueberries on one half, and fold over the tortilla to close.

Over medium heat, grill for 2 minutes on each side, until the quesadilla crisps and blueberries heat through.

Transfer the quesadilla to a cutting board and use a pizza cutter to slice into triangles. Serve.

YIELD: 1 to 2 servings

Spinach and Artichoke Cups

This is one of our MOMables member favorite mini meals. The bite-size pieces bring the ultimate kid appeal to eating your veggies.

24 wonton wrappers, at room temperature

6 ounces (168 g) artichoke hearts, drained and roughly chopped

10 ounces (280 g) frozen chopped spinach, thawed and squeezed dry

1 cup (115 g) shredded Monterey Jack cheese

½ cup (50 g) grated Parmesan cheese

¼ cup (60 g) cream cheese, softened

¼ cup (60 g) plain Greek yogurt

1 garlic clove, minced

Preheat the oven to 350°F (180°C). Spray mini cupcake pan with cooking spray.

Gently place one wonton wrapper into each mini cupcake cup, pressing down to bring it to the bottom.

In the bowl of a food processor, insert artichoke hearts, spinach, cheeses, Greek yogurt, and garlic. Pulse a few times to combine. You can also combine all the ingredients in a large bowl and mix thoroughly using a fork.

Spoon 1 tablespoon (20 g) of spinach artichoke mixture into each wonton wrapper cup.

Bake spinach artichoke cups for about 10 minutes, or until golden brown and crispy on the edges.

YIELD: 24 servings

DIY Nachos ▷

This fun snack is a thousand times better than the nacho tray sold at sporting events, but it retains all the sentiment of the classic snack.

1 bag (16 ounces, or 454 g) corn tortilla chips

1½ cups (356 g) Momveeta Cheese (page 144) or 1½ cups (175 g) shredded cheese

Toppings of choice, such as black beans, leftover grilled chicken, diced tomatoes, black olives, jalapeños, or guacamole

Place the oven rack in the bottom third of the oven and preheat the oven to a low broil. Line two baking sheets with parchment paper.

Distribute corn tortilla chips evenly onto both baking sheets or create 4 to 6 individual mounds of chips.

Pour warm Momveeta or shredded cheese evenly over all the chips, top with desired toppings, and broil for 2 to 3 minutes. Remove from the oven and serve immediately.

YIELD: 4 to 6 servings

Laura's Tip

For a video tutorial, see http://bit.ly/nachonight.

Tex-Mex Chicken Salad Bites

I made this Tex-Mex salad for a party and I couldn't keep everyone out of the fridge. It was gone before I served it.

2 tablespoons (30 g) plain Greek yogurt

Juice from 1 small lime

1 avocado, divided

Pinch of salt

Pinch of cumin powder

1 cup (140 g) cooked chicken, diced small

1 cup (150 g) frozen corn kernels

¼ cup (45 g) cherry tomatoes, diced

½ cup (8 g) chopped fresh cilantro

2 tablespoons (30 ml) fresh salsa

Homemade Tortilla Chips (page 121) for serving

In a small bowl, combine yogurt, lime juice, half of an avocado, salt, and cumin. Mash all ingredients together until creamy (you can also do this in a blender for a more even consistency).

In a large bowl, combine chicken, corn, cherry tomatoes, cilantro, and fresh salsa. Fold in creamy yogurt dressing until evenly combined. Refrigerate for 1 hour.

Serve with tortilla chips.

YIELD: 4 servings

Southwest Chicken Salad

You can make awesome snacks with leftover chicken. Whether you stuff this salad in a pita, wrap it up in a tortilla, or eat it with Homemade Tortilla Chips (page 121), this recipe is a winner.

1 cup (230 g) plain Greek yogurt

1 teaspoon taco seasoning

2 chicken breasts, cooked and diced

2 small tomatoes, diced

1 red pepper, diced

1 can (15 ounces, or 425 g) black beans, drained and rinsed

2 cups (510 g) corn

2 tablespoons (20 g) green onions, chopped

In a large bowl, mix yogurt and taco seasoning.

Add diced chicken, tomatoes, red pepper, black beans, corn, and green onions to the yogurt mixture. Toss all ingredients thoroughly to coat well.

Refrigerate for 1 hour and serve.

YIELD: 4 to 6 servings

Ninja Turtle Nuggets

These broccoli and cheese nuggets are so good, I guarantee nobody will complain about eating their vegetables.

1 pound (455 g) broccoli florets

1 cup (115 g) breadcrumbs

1 teaspoon Italian seasoning

1½ cups (173 g) shredded cheddar cheese

3 large eggs

Steam broccoli until it is tender but still slightly crisp. Rinse under cold water to stop the cooking process and set aside.

Preheat the oven to 375°F (190°C) and line a baking pan with parchment paper or a silicone mat.

In a large bowl, mix breadcrumbs, Italian seasoning, and cheddar cheese.

In the bowl of a food processor, pulse broccoli florets until they are finely chopped, then add the broccoli to the bowl and mix thoroughly. Add eggs and combine.

Using an ice cream scoop or your hands, shape nuggets into round shapes on a baking pan. Press down with your hands to flatten.

Bake for 20 to 25 minutes, turning the nuggets over after 15 minutes.

YIELD: 4 to 6 servings

- -

KITCHEN NOTE

Make nuggets gluten free by using gluten-free breadcrumbs.

- -

Baked Zucchini Bites

This recipe has bite-size appeal for kids and the healthy ingredients I'm looking for in a portable snack. Best of all, it's perfectly delicious warm or cold.

2 cups (220 g) zucchini, grated

2 eggs, whisked

½ cup (80 g) onion, diced

1 clove garlic, minced

½ cup (58 g) cheddar cheese, shredded

½ cup (60 g) panko breadcrumbs

½ teaspoon salt

¼ teaspoon pepper

1 cup (245 g) marinara or other sauce, for dipping

Preheat the oven to 400°F (200°C) and grease a mini muffin tin.

Season the zucchini with a pinch of salt and place in the middle of a piece of cheesecloth or on a thin kitchen towel. Pat dry to absorb all liquid, wring it out, and transfer into a large bowl.

To the shredded zucchini, add the eggs, onion, garlic, cheese, panko breadcrumbs, salt, and pepper. Stir until evenly combined.

Scoop the mixture into the mini muffin tin, filling each well to the top. Bake for 15 to 18 minutes, or until golden. Allow the zucchini bites to cool slightly before transferring to a wire rack to cool. Serve with marinara or your favorite dipping sauce.

YIELD: 24 bite-size pieces

- -

KITCHEN NOTE

Make these zucchini bites gluten free by substituting the panko breadcrumbs with crushed rice cereal.

- -

CHAPTER 7

- - - - - - - - - - - -

SUPER SMOOTHIES AND DRINKS

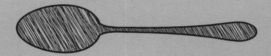

"It's a smoothie! It's a milkshake! It has superpowers!" That was my ritual chant to my kids when they gave me the skeptical look about what came out of the blender. Over time, they've found that even the most nutritious smoothies can often taste like dessert. Let's raise our glasses to more fruits and veggies, shall we?

◀ Elvis Shakes

If you could only imagine my middle son at the age of 3, lip-synching to Elvis while pretending that the straw in this smoothie was a microphone, you'd understand exactly how this shake got its name.

2 large bananas, sliced and frozen

1½ cups (360 ml) milk

6 tablespoons (96 g) creamy peanut butter

2 tablespoons (42 g) honey

¼ teaspoon cinnamon

¾ cup (170 g) crushed ice cubes

Place milk and bananas in the blender and pulse a few times to combine.

Add peanut butter, honey, cinnamon, and crushed ice. Blend until smooth.

Pour into 4 glasses, add straws, and serve.

YIELD: 4 servings

Banana Blueberry Orange Smoothie

When bananas go beyond ripe in our house, I slice them up, put them in a sealable freezer bag, and freeze them for quick and easy smoothies such as this one. The frozen fruit will give you a thick smoothie consistency kids love.

½ cup (120 ml) almond milk

1 medium orange, peeled, halved

1 small banana, peeled, sliced, and frozen

½ cup (75 g) unsweetened blueberries, frozen

In a blender, combine almond milk, orange, banana, and frozen blueberries.

Blend until smooth.

YIELD: 1 serving

Berry Banana Smoothie

"Mom! Where did you buy this milkshake from?" asked my daughter, Sofia, age 7. This is proof that not all the thick, delicious, ice-creamlike smoothies require a trip to the nearest fast-food chain.

½ cup (40 g) old-fashioned oats

1½ cups (355 ml) almond milk

2 large overly ripe bananas, peeled, sliced, and frozen

1 cup (145 g) strawberries, frozen

1 cup (225 g) ice

Pulse oats in a blender several times to break down.

Add almond milk, bananas, strawberries, and ice. Blend until smooth.

YIELD: 2 servings

Mango Peach Smoothie

If you love tropical, sweet smoothies, look no further. Simply make this recipe and enjoy.

1½ cups (355 ml) almond milk

1 cup (170 g) peaches, sliced and frozen

1 cup (175 g) mango, chopped and frozen

½ teaspoon vanilla extract

1 cup ice

In a blender combine almond milk, peaches, mango, and vanilla. Blend well.

Add ice and continue to blend until smooth. If it's too thick, add a little more almond milk.

YIELD: 2 servings

Summer Blush Smoothie

I am known for buying an excessive amount of grapes when they are in season. One day I decided to use them up in a smoothie and now it's become my go-to method of pretending I didn't buy too many.

2 cups (475 ml) water

2 cups (300 g) grapes

2 cups (340 g) unsweetened peaches, frozen

1 cup (255 g) strawberries, frozen

1 banana

In a blender combine water, grapes, peaches, strawberries, and banana. Blend well until smooth.

YIELD: 4 servings

What Type of Blender is Best?

I'm often asked what type of blender is best to create very smooth and consistent smoothies. The truth is that I still own a $20 (£12.50) blender from fifteen years ago, a $100 (£62.50) blender from our wedding registry, and two high-end $400 (£250) blenders. They all "blend," but here are my thoughts on blender basics:

• Inexpensive blenders are good for salad dressings, dips, and simple smoothies. Most models leave crushed pieces of ice behind and never blend leafy greens well.

• Middle-of-the road models are better at crushing ice and making sure frozen fruit is thoroughly incorporated. Some leave leafy pieces behind—something my kids don't like.

• Commercial-grade blenders are more expensive but worth the investment if you use them often. It wasn't until I purchased a high-end blender that my family began drinking green smoothies. Now it's the most used appliance I own and it sits on my counter at all times.

• The key is to purchase a blender that will fit your needs. Borrow one from a friend for a couple of days and see how you like his or her particular model.

Raisin Paste

Raisins are naturally sweet, and they have antioxidants, fiber, and potassium. I love using raisin paste as a substitute for dates, which tend to be more expensive. I store a small jar in my fridge at all times. It is such a great addition to smoothies; I call for it in my Super Hero Smoothie (page 187), Super Green Smoothie (page 187), Apple Quinoa Smoothie (page 188), and Antioxidant Smoothie (page 189), but you can use it as a natural sweetener in many recipes.

1½ cups (247 g) dried raisins

2½ cups (587 ml) boiling water

Place raisins in a glass bowl. Pour just enough boiling water on top to cover the raisins. Set aside for 10 minutes or so to rehydrate the raisins into plump fruit. Reserve ¼ cup (60 ml) raisin water and drain.

Transfer raisins into a food processor or blender. Blend until the raisins make a thick paste. Add water, 1 tablespoon (15 ml) at a time, until you have a smooth peanut-butterlike consistency.

Store in the refrigerator for up to 3 weeks. You can also freeze raisin paste cubes and store them in freezer bags for months.

YIELD: Approximately 1 cup (250 g)

Laura's Tip

Use raisin paste as you would typically use honey in smoothies, to sweeten plain yogurt, and even in oatmeal!

Super Hero Smoothie

For the kid who already loves green smoothies, this one is loaded with super powers. Not only is it packed with fiber and vitamin C, it's also a refreshing healthy treat.

1 cup (235 ml) water or apple juice

2 cups (60 g) loosely packed spinach

2 tablespoons (8 g) chopped parsley

1 Granny Smith apple, halved, cored, and cut into large chunks

1 piece (3-inches, or 2.5 cm) fresh ginger, peeled and coarsely chopped

1 tablespoon (20 g) Raisin Paste (page 185)

1 cup (225 g) ice

In a blender, place water or apple juice, spinach, parsley, apple, ginger, Raisin Paste, and ice.

Blend well, stopping a few times to make sure greens get incorporated thoroughly.

YIELD: 2 servings

Super Green Smoothie

My neighbor used to buy the super green smoothie from the grocery store. One day, we looked at the ingredients and created our own.

2½ cups (570 ml) almond milk

2 tablespoons (40 g) Raisin Paste (page 185)

1 banana

1 cup (67 g) chopped kale leaves

1 cup (30 g) spinach

1 cup (145 g) frozen berries of any kind

In a blender place almond milk, Raisin Paste, banana, kale, spinach, and berries.

Blend until smooth.

YIELD: 2 servings

Tropical Smoothie

Whenever I'm lucky enough to sip the last drops of this smoothie right out of the blender's pitcher, I close my eyes and imagine I'm laying on a beach somewhere. That last sip is 10 seconds of imaginary peace in my busy world of mom.

¾ cup (173 g) vanilla yogurt

1½ cups (353 ml) coconut milk

1½ cups (250 g) frozen pineapple chunks

1 large banana

1 cup (225 g) crushed ice

Place yogurt, coconut milk, frozen pineapple chunks, and banana inside a blender. Pulse a few times to combine, then and add crushed ice.

Blend until smooth.

YIELD: 4 servings

Laura's Tip

Place soft and liquid ingredients at the bottom of the blender for easier blending and the frozen and harder ingredients toward the top.

Apple Quinoa Smoothie

Not knowing what to do with that serving of leftover quinoa can be a tragedy sometimes. One day, I decided to throw it in the blender for additional protein and fiber. The result was a delicious and much thicker smoothie than usual. My kids call this the apple pie shake.

2 cups (475 ml) milk

¾ cup (139 g) cold cooked quinoa

2 apples, diced

2 tablespoons (32 g) Raisin Paste (page 185)

½ teaspoon cinnamon

1 teaspoon vanilla extract

1 cup (225 g) ice cubes

Place milk, quinoa, apples, Raisin Paste, cinnamon, vanilla extract, and ice in a blender. Pulse a few times and blend until smooth.

YIELD: 4 servings

Antioxidant Smoothie

I usually buy a large bottle of pomegranate juice to use in my Homemade Icy Drink recipe (page 194). In order to use up the extra juice before it spoils, I make this delicious smoothie my kids love.

1½ cups (355 ml) unsweetened pomegranate juice

1 cup (145 g) frozen blueberries

2 tablespoons (14 g) flax meal

2 tablespoons (40 g) Raisin Paste (page 185)

½ cup (115 g) yogurt

1 cup (225 g) ice

Place juice, blueberries, flax meal, Raisan Paste, yogurt, and ice inside a blender. Pulse a few times and blend until smooth.

YIELD: 2 servings

Laura's Tip

If the pomegranate juice is too tart, try using blueberry juice or dark grape juice. Dark, colorful fruits contain the most antioxidants.

Thick and Creamy Dairy-Free Yogurt

For those of us with kids who can't have dairy, this is an affordable yogurt substitute. It's a great base for parfait recipes, topped with granola, or enjoyed as is.

2 tablespoons (30 ml) warm water

1½ teaspoons powdered gelatin

2 cups (475 ml) unsweetened vanilla almond milk

2 tablespoons (30 ml) maple syrup or honey

Place warm water and gelatin in a small bowl. Stir to combine and let it sit for 10 minutes to form a jellylike mixture.

Meanwhile, in a medium saucepan, whisk almond milk and maple syrup or honey.

Warm milk until nearly to the boiling point, stirring often. Remove from heat.

Add ¼ cup (60 ml) warm milk to the gelatin mixture and whisk until it completely dissolves. Pour gelatin mixture into the saucepan and whisk to combine.

Fill four 6-ounce (175 ml) glass ramekins or mason jars with yogurt mixture. Allow yogurts to cool to room temperature, cover, and refrigerate overnight.

YIELD: 4 servings

Laura's Tip

I sometimes mix half canned coconut milk and half almond milk for a more nutritious yogurt. For a nut-free recipe, this also works with rice milk.

Homemade Yogurt Drink

My son can't get enough of those drinkable yogurts from the grocery store. He loves them, but I don't love the ingredients, or the cost! My homemade version is delicious, has real fruit, and is cheaper!

2 cups (475 ml) milk

½ cup (115 g) yogurt

2 tablespoons (30 ml) maple syrup or honey

1 cup (145 g) chopped fruit

Place all ingredients in a blender and blend on medium-low until everything is smooth and evenly combined.

Pour yogurt drinks in 4-ounce (120 ml) drink containers and refrigerate for 1 hour prior to serving.

YIELD: 4 servings

KITCHEN NOTE

The honey or maple syrup is optional in both the Diary-Free Yogurt and Homemade Yogurt Drink recipes.

Laura's Tip

Have leftover yogurt drink? Freeze into popsicles for later!

Homemade Hot Chocolate

With dozens of praising comments on MOMables, this is one of the most searched-for recipes in the wintertime.

¼ cup (20 g) unsweetened cocoa powder

½ cup (115 g) granulated sugar

⅓ cup (80 ml) hot water

⅛ teaspoon salt

4 cups (940 ml) milk

1 teaspoon vanilla

Combine the cocoa, sugar, water, and salt in a medium saucepan. Over medium-high heat, stir constantly until the mixture boils. Reduce heat to low and cook, stirring for 1 minute. Stir in the milk making sure the chocolate is thoroughly combined and heat up your milk but do not boil.

Remove hot chocolate from heat and add in vanilla, stir. Serve immediately.

YIELD: 4 servings

- -

KITCHEN NOTE

You can substitute granulated sugar with honey or maple syrup in this recipe. For a dairy-free version, use nondairy milk. The results are just as delicious.

- -

Homemade Sports Drink

What's the point of buying drinks with artificial colors and high fructose corn syrup when you can make your own with better ingredients?

3 cups (705 ml) cold water

1 cup (235 ml) pineapple juice

¾ teaspoon sea salt

⅛ teaspoon baking soda

In a pitcher, combine water, pineapple juice, sea salt, and baking soda.

Refrigerate until cold. Serve over ice.

YIELD: 4 servings

Laura's Tip

If your child is playing strenuous sports or under extreme heat, you can purchase bottled water with added electrolytes. Use that water to make the recipe for an additional boost of electrolytes.

DIY Hot Cocoa Mix

Exactly like the store-bought packets, but homemade.

1 cup (80 g) cocoa powder

2 cups (240 g) powdered sugar

2½ cups (300 g) powdered milk

1 teaspoon salt

2 teaspoons cornstarch

Combine everything in a large bowl or food processor, mix well, and store in an airtight container or zip-top bag.

To make hot cocoa, place ⅓ to ½ cup (45 to 60 g) of the mix into a mug and fill with 1 cup (235 ml) hot water. Stir well until fully dissolved.

YIELD: 6 to 8 servings

Real Fruit Punch

My kids tried the red fruit punch at a birthday party and loved it. Wanting to avoid artificial colors and additives, I made my own.

2 cups (470 ml) apple juice, chilled

2 cups (470 ml) grape juice, chilled

½ cup (120 ml) pineapple juice

1 tablespoon (15 ml) lime juice

3 cups (705 ml) carbonated water

Ice

In a large pitcher, combine apple juice, grape juice, pineapple juice, and lime juice. Add carbonated water and stir.

Add ice and serve.

YIELD: Approximately eight 1-cup (235 ml) servings

Homemade Icy Drink ▶

The original drink is full of sugar and artificial colors, two things that are sure to give my kids an extra dose of unnatural energy. My version is simple and my kids love it.

2 cups (475 ml) crushed ice

⅔ cup (157 ml) 100 percent fruit juice

In a blender combine ice and fruit juice. Blend until you have an even slush consistency and no chunks of ice remain.

Pour into glasses and enjoy immediately.

YIELD: 2 servings

Laura's Tip

I've found my kids prefer this icy drink made with grape juice, pomegranate juice, blueberry juice, and cherry juice. The outcome is a darker icy drink, very similar to the ones sold at the convenience store.

◄ OJ Cubes

Fake-flavored water? I don't think so! These fun ice cubes are all you need to get your kids to drink more water.

2 cups (455 g) frozen orange juice concentrate

Thaw frozen orange juice concentrate, pour it into ice-cube trays, and freeze for 8 hours or overnight.

Place 2 to 4 OJ Cubes into an 8-ounce (240 ml) glass of fresh, filtered water and enjoy.

YIELD: 4 to 6 servings

Fruit Ice Cubes

While these aren't technically a snack, people often ask me how I get my kids to drink more water. The answer is to make it appealing. My daughter loves how pretty these cubes make her glass. Add a straw and sip away!

1 cup (145 g) mixed berries, washed and sliced

Water

Place berries inside an ice-cube tray and add enough water to fill the tray. Freeze until solid.

YIELD: 12 to 16 cubes, depending on tray size

Raspberry Green Tea

My daughter is the tea drinker in our house. She loves it when I use fresh fruit to flavor her tea.

2 cups (250 g) fresh raspberries

1 cup (235 ml) plus 1 quart (946 ml) filtered water, divided

⅓ cup (107 g) honey

4 green tea bags

1 quart (946 ml) filtered water

Ice, for serving

In a medium saucepan, combine raspberries, 1 cup (235 ml) water, and honey; bring to a boil. Reduce heat and simmer, until the berries begin to break down, about 7 minutes.

Over a heat-proof bowl, strain the berry mixture through a sieve, pressing down with a spoon.

Brew tea bags in 1 quart (946 ml) of boiling water, allowing the green tea to steep for 2 to 3 minutes. Discard tea bags and allow tea to cool.

In fill a large pitcher with iced water, brewed tea, and raspberry mixture. Pour tea over ice.

YIELD: 8 servings

Homemade Lemonade

My friend Alison shared her favorite lemonade recipe when my kids wanted to do a lemonade stand. I'm not sure if we sold more than we drank ourselves, but in the end, the recipe was a huge success.

1 cup (235 ml) water

1 cup (200 g) sugar (or honey)

1 cup (235 ml) lemon juice, freshly squeezed

6 cups (1.4 L) cold water

Ice

In a small saucepan, bring the water and sugar to a boil until the sugar is dissolved, creating a simple syrup. Remove from heat and allow simple syrup to cool.

Inside a large pitcher, pour freshly squeezed lemon juice, simple syrup, and cold water. Add ice or refrigerate until cold, about 1 hour.

If lemonade is too sweet add additional lemon juice or dilute with water.

YIELD: 8 servings

Lemonade Granita

My daughter, a huge lemonade fan, loves taking this to summer camp in her insulated drink mug for an added treat and summer chill.

2 cups (475 ml) Homemade Lemonade (at left)

6 cups (1.4 kg) ice

In a blender combine lemonade and ice. Blend until you have an even slush consistency and no chunks of ice remain.

Pour into glasses and enjoy immediately.

YIELD: 6 servings

Blackberry Ginger Lemonade

In the summer, when blackberries are plentiful, I like to add a little flavor to our lemonade ... naturally.

6 cups (1.4 L) water, divided

1 cup (200 g) sugar

1½ cups (220 g) blackberries

1 teaspoon fresh ginger, grated

1 cup (235 ml) lemon juice, freshly squeezed

Ice

In a small saucepan, bring 1 cup (235 ml) water, sugar, blackberries, and ginger to a boil until sugar is dissolved, continuously mashing the blackberries to incorporate them into a simple syrup. Remove from heat and allow the mixture to cool.

Strain the simple syrup through a colander and into a large pitcher, pressing down to release all the blackberry juices. Pour freshly squeezed lemon juice, remaining water, and ice into the pitcher. Stir to combine and serve.

YIELD: 8 servings

- -

KITCHEN NOTE

Frozen blackberries work well in this recipe too!

- -

Strawberry Lemonade ▶

I love making pitchers full of strawberry lemonade to share with friends or bring to the park. When we have leftovers, I make little ice cubes that I use to flavor water.

2 cups (340 g) strawberries, sliced

¾ cup (255 g) honey

1 cup (235 ml) freshly squeezed lemon juice

4 cups (940 ml) water

Ice cubes for serving

In a blender or food processor, purée the strawberries and honey.

Pour the strawberry purée into a pitcher. Stir in lemon juice and water.

Serve over ice.

YIELD: 8 servings

CHAPTER 8

- - - - - - - - - - -

FROZEN DELIGHTS AND SPECIAL TREATS

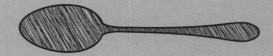

I've never heard one of my kids say "No" to trying one of my homemade ice creams. Once I learned how easy it is to turn fruit into ice cream, I got really creative.

Of course, my "Let's turn fruit into something frozen" plan didn't end there. The popsicles in this book are always a huge success with my kids.

Chocolate Hazelnut Banana Ice Cream

This ice cream is so, so good, and you won't believe how easy it is to make!

2 bananas, sliced and frozen

3 tablespoons (27 g) Homemade Chocolate Hazelnut Spread (at right)

In a food processor, pulse frozen bananas to break into small chunks, then turn it on until you have the consistency of soft-serve ice cream. Add the chocolate hazelnut spread and pulse to combine. Transfer to a freezer-safe container and chill for at least 1 hour before serving.

YIELD: 2 servings

Cinnamon Dulce Banana Ice Cream

My grandmother used to make a dulce de leche ice cream that was out of this world. One day, I decided to take our favorite easy ice cream recipe for a spin and create hers. It was love at first taste.

4 medium bananas, frozen

⅓ cup (101 g) sweetened condensed milk

1 teaspoon cinnamon

In a food processor, pulse frozen bananas to break into small chunks, then turn it on until you have the consistency of soft-serve ice cream.

Add the condensed milk and cinnamon, and pulse to combine. Transfer to a freezer-safe container and chill for at least 1 hour before serving.

YIELD: 4 servings

Homemade Chocolate Hazelnut Spread

2 cups (270 g) hazelnuts, skins removed

3 tablespoons (15 g) unsweetened cocoa powder

3 tablespoons (45 ml) melted coconut oil

¼ cup (50 ml) pure maple syrup

1 teaspoon vanilla

Pinch of salt

Preheat oven to 300°F (150°C). Spread peeled hazelnuts on a baking sheet and roast for 10 minutes, stopping to give them a quick toss half way through. Remove from oven and transfer them to the bowl of your food processor.

To the hazelnuts, add cocoa powder, melted coconut oil, maple syrup, vanilla, and salt. Turn food processor on for 5 to 7 minutes or until it yields a thick creamy mixture.

Transfer hazelnut spread to an airtight container and refrigerate.

YIELD: 1½ cups (390 g)

- -

KITCHEN NOTE

If spread is too thick after 10 minutes of continuous mixing, add a teaspoon (5 ml) of melted coconut oil at a time until desired consistency is achieved. The chocolate hazelnut mixture will spread easiest at room temperature.

- -

Aloha Ice Cream Pops

I once doubled the Aloha cups recipe and saved leftovers for later. The next day I came up with this easy variation my kids loved!

1 recipe Aloha Cups (page 33)

2 cups (460 g) vanilla yogurt

Prepare Aloha Cups recipe and allow it to cool to room temperature.

In a blender, mix Aloha Cups mixture and vanilla yogurt. Pour into ice cream pop molds. Freeze for 4 to 6 hours and enjoy.

YIELD: 6 to 8 servings

Mango Freeze Pops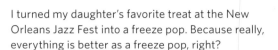

I turned my daughter's favorite treat at the New Orleans Jazz Fest into a freeze pop. Because really, everything is better as a freeze pop, right?

1 cup (235 ml) coconut milk

2 tablespoons (30 ml) maple syrup (optional)

3 cups (525 g) mango chunks

Purée the coconut milk, maple syrup (if using), and mango in a blender until smooth. Increase speed to the highest setting and whip the mixture for 1 minute.

Pour the whipped mango blend into freezer pops, freeze for 6 hours or until solid, and enjoy.

YIELD: 8 freeze pops

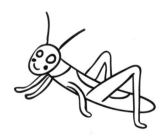

Strawberry Yogurt Freeze Pops

The first time I made these, I served them to my kids for breakfast. They were shocked. With an eyebrow raised, I thought to myself, "It's just strawberries and yogurt." There is nothing wrong with making breakfast more fun!

1½ cups (345 g) vanilla Greek yogurt

1½ cups (255 g) strawberries, sliced

In a large bowl, combine yogurt and fruit.

Spoon yogurt mix inside freezer pop molds. Freeze until firm.

YIELD: 6 freeze pops

Frozen Yogurt Blueberry Bites

In the summer, I pack a few of these inside a thermos container for camp snack. My kids love the slushy texture. Of course, we also enjoy them right out of the freezer.

2 cups (460 g) vanilla Greek yogurt

1½ cups (220 g) blueberries

In a large bowl combine yogurt and blueberries, mixing gently with a spatula.

Pour yogurt mixture into 2 or 3 ice cube trays. Freeze for 2 or 3 hours or overnight. Remove from the tray and serve.

YIELD: 4 to 6 servings

Easy Strawberries and Cream Ice Cream

You know those frozen strawberries you've forgotten about in the back of the freezer? They are perfect for this simple ice cream recipe.

2 bananas, peeled and frozen

½ cup (127 g) strawberries, frozen

3 tablespoons (45 ml) heavy cream

In a food processor or high speed blender, blend bananas, strawberry chunks, and cream until they are the consistency of soft-serve ice cream.

Transfer mixture to a freezer-safe container and freeze until solid.

Scoop the ice cream with an ice cream scoop and serve.

YIELD: 2 servings

Peanut Butter and Honey Banana Ice Cream

After tasting this ice cream for the first time, my daughter Sofia, age 4, said, "When Tigger and Pooh have a party, this ice cream is served."

2 large bananas, peeled and frozen

¼ cup (65 g) peanut butter

1 tablespoon (20 g) honey

In a food processor, blend bananas until they resemble chunks. Add peanut butter and honey, and blend until it becomes soft serve ice cream.

Serve as is or freeze for 1 hour and use an ice cream scoop to form balls.

YIELD: 2 servings

Laura's Tip

Add a dash of cinnamon or top with shredded coconut for extra deliciousness.

Monkey Ice Cream Sandwiches

These are the easiest ice cream sandwiches you'll ever make.

2 large ripe bananas

3 tablespoons (48 g) crunchy peanut butter

16 Homemade Graham Cracker squares (page 142)

Peel the bananas and place in a small bowl. Add crunchy peanut butter and mash together using a fork until creamy.

Spread about 1 tablespoon (20 g) of the mixture onto one side of 8 graham crackers. Top with remaining graham crackers to make sandwiches.

On a parchment paper–lined baking sheet, place graham sandwiches. Freeze for 4 hours and serve.

YIELD: 8 ice cream sandwiches

Strawberry Cheesecake Ice Cream Sandwiches

I love making these sandwiches for parties or large playdates. They are always a hit with the kids, and the large pan serves many!

2 cups (340 g) diced strawberries

12 to 16 Homemade Graham Crackers (page 142)

8 ounces (225 g) cream cheese

24 ounces (690 g) plain Greek yogurt

1 tablespoon (15 ml) vanilla

3 tablespoons (60 g) honey or maple syrup

Wash and chop strawberries, place them on a cookie sheet, and place in the freezer for 30 minutes. Place graham crackers on another cookie sheet and freeze for about 30 minutes. In your stand mixer (or large bowl) combine cream cheese, Greek yogurt, and vanilla. Once combined, add the honey (or maple syrup, if using). Fold semi-frozen berries into yogurt mixture.

Line a 13 × 9-inch (33 × 23 cm) baking dish with parchment paper. Break each graham cracker in half and cover the bottom of the dish with a single layer of graham crackers. Reserve remaining ones for later. Pour strawberry yogurt mixture on top of graham crackers. Add second layer of graham crackers on top for top crust.

Freeze tray for about 4 hours. When ready to eat, lift parchment paper and cut through with a sharp knife to create individual sandwiches.

Serve immediately or wrap individual servings in plastic wrap until ready to serve.

YIELD: 12 servings

Pineapple Whip Ice Cream

My favorite ice cream is the pineapple soft serve sold at Disneyworld. Since we can't go to Disneyworld every time I'm in the mood for one, I've made my own version.

20 ounces (566 g) crushed pineapple

13 ounces (385 ml) canned coconut milk

2 tablespoons (30 ml) maple syrup

In a blender, combine crushed pineapple, coconut milk, and maple syrup and mix until smooth. Continue blending, increasing the power to high for 1 minute.

Pour mixture into an ice cream maker, process for about 20 minutes or until it's thick and creamy. Alternatively, you can freeze mixture in a 9 × 5-inch (23 × 13 cm) bread pan for 4 to 6 hours until frozen. Use an ice cream scoop to serve.

YIELD: 6 servings

Banana Split Freeze Pops

Here it is—all the awesome flavors of the decadent dessert bar, in every lick.

2 cups (460 g) vanilla yogurt

2 tablespoons (32 g) peanut butter

1 large banana, chopped

½ cup (88 g) mini chocolate chips

½ cup (160 g) Strawberry Freezer Jam (page 56)

In a large bowl, add vanilla yogurt, peanut butter, chopped banana, chocolate chips, and strawberry jam, stirring with a wooden spoon to combine.

Holding a freeze pop mold with one hand and a spoon in the other, begin filling each popsicle mold, leaving some space for the lid.

Freeze for 6 hours or until solid.

YIELD: 6 to 8 freeze pops

Chocolate Super Pops

Healthy dark chocolate fudgy pops? Yes, please! And these have only 2 tablespoons (40 g) honey (for the whole batch!).

2 ripe avocados, pitted and peeled

1 very ripe banana, peeled

2 tablespoons (10 g) plus 1 teaspoon (2 g) of cocoa powder

2 tablespoons (40 g) honey

¾ cup (175 ml) milk

½ teaspoon vanilla extract

Put all ingredients into a food processor or blender and mix until smooth, stopping throughout to scrape the sides.

Pour the mixture into freeze pop molds and freeze for 4 hours or until solid.

YIELD: 6 to 8 freeze pops

Green Super Pops

Who says you can't get the kids to eat more greens? These are a treat your kids will love!

1 cup (165 g) pineapple chunks

1 large handful spinach leaves

1 cup (230 g) vanilla Greek yogurt

Place pineapple chunks, spinach, and yogurt inside a blender. Blend on high until thoroughly combined.

Transfer green mixture into 4 freeze pop molds. Freeze until solid.

YIELD: 4 servings

Fresh Fruit and Lemonade Pops

For this recipe, I love using kiwis, blueberries, strawberries, and anything that will look pretty in the freeze pop. My kids think they are eating a rainbow!

2 cups (475 ml) Homemade Lemonade (page 199)

1½ cups (245 g) fresh fruit, sliced

Place your choice of fresh, sliced fruit into each pop mold, filling it nearly to the top but not stuffing it tightly.

Pour lemonade into each mold, covering the fruit and leaving a little room at the top for expansion.

Freeze for at least 6 hours or overnight.

YIELD: 6 to 8 freeze pops

Kiwi Ice Cream

Loaded with vitamin C and potassium, this is my go-to ice cream when my kids are home with the sniffles and want a treat.

2 bananas, frozen

4 kiwis, peeled and sliced

In a food processor, pulse frozen bananas to break into small chunks. Add kiwi slices and turn it on until you have the consistency of soft-serve ice cream.

Transfer to a freezer-safe container and freeze for at least 1 hour before serving.

YIELD: 4 servings

Homemade Almond Butter Cups

Once in a while, this mom *needs chocolate* and the almond butter plus chocolate combination is my favorite. Of course, these can also be made with nut-free butter.

2 cups (350 g) chocolate chips

½ cup (130 g) smooth almond butter

¼ cup (15 g) powdered sugar

1 tablespoon (14 g) butter, melted

Melt chocolate chips in a double boiler or in the microwave, stirring frequently.

Meanwhile, combine almond butter, powdered sugar, and butter in a bowl. Refrigerate for 10 minutes.

Line a 12-cup muffin pan with paper liners. Spoon about a teaspoon, (or just enough to cover the bottom), of chocolate into the bottom of each paper liner. Once all 12 are filled, refrigerate for about 10 minutes, or until the chocolate sets.

Remove the cupcake pan and almond butter mixture from the fridge.

Spoon 1 heaping teaspoon of almond butter mixture on top of the chocolate layers, spreading evenly using the back of a spoon.

Top almond butter layer with another teaspoon or so of melted chocolate. Repeat process with remaining cups and refrigerate for 30 minutes, or until all the layers have fully set.

YIELD: 12 servings

Trail Mix Bites ▷

Crunchy chocolate? Yes please! This is my version of a candy bar.

¼ cup (35 g) trail mix (any from this cookbook)

¼ cup (44 g) dark chocolate chips

In a double boiler or microwave, melt chocolate. If using the microwave to melt, place in a microwave-safe bowl and stir every 15 to 20 seconds.

Line a baking pan with a piece of wax paper and pour 2 teaspoons of melted chocolate onto the pan, spreading it into a thin layer to create a 1-inch (2.5 cm) base.

Sprinkle or place 2 teaspoons of trail mix pieces evenly over the chocolate base. Press each nut or fruit down lightly to secure in place.

Repeat this process until you have a total of 6 chocolate bases.

Refrigerate pan for 30 minutes or until set.

YIELD: 6 servings

Coconut Almond Bites

I made these as a teacher appreciation gift one year and wrapped them up inside a cute cellophane bag. If you are making them for the entire class, be certain there are no nut allergies in the classroom.

1¼ cups (100 g) shredded coconut

¼ cup (60 ml) condensed milk

½ teaspoon vanilla

2 cups (350 g) dark chocolate chunks

36 roasted almonds

36 mini cupcake pan liners

In a large bowl, mix shredded coconut, condensed milk, and vanilla. The mixture will be sticky but pliable enough for you to shape.

In a double boiler, melt the chocolate.

Fill a mini cupcake pan with paper liners (I find that the treats hold up better this way).

Add a teaspoon or so of melted chocolate into the bottom of each cup, or enough to fill the bottom. Top with a teaspoon of coconut mixture and press down lightly using your spoon.

Top the coconut with an almond, pressing it down to sink into the coconut slightly, and top with more melted chocolate, enough to cover.

Repeat this process with the remaining mixture and chocolate, and refrigerate for 20 minutes to set.

YIELD: 30 to 36 pieces

Frosty Treats

During Halloween, one of my neighbors hands out little coupons for this popular restaurant treat. When those few treat vouchers run out, I'm left making my own version at home. My kids love it!

¼ cup (60 ml) milk

2½ cups (370 g) vanilla ice cream, softened

¼ cup (65 g) Homemade Chocolate Hazelnut Spread (page 205)

In a blender, combine milk, vanilla ice cream, and Chocolate Hazelnut Spread.

Pour into individual cups and serve with a spoon.

YIELD: 4 servings

Chocolate Covered PB&J Bites

My son used to love peanut butter and jelly cracker sandwiches for snack. One day, I was in charge of bringing a classroom treat and I simply upped the "treat factor" of one of his favorite snacks by dipping them in chocolate.

¾ cup (120 g) creamy peanut butter or nut-free alternative

½ cup (160 g) strawberry jam

60 whole-wheat round crackers

1¼ cups (219 g) semisweet chocolate chips

1¼ cups (219 g) white chocolate chips

Line a baking pan with parchment paper.

Spread peanut butter onto half of the crackers, top with jam, and gently cover each with another cracker.

Put the semisweet chocolate in a microwave-safe bowl and melt in 30-second intervals, stirring well between each interval, until completely smooth. Or, you can melt chocolate in a double boiler.

Use a spoon to gently dunk 15 of the cracker sandwiches, tapping off any extra chocolate. Transfer covered sandwiches to the prepared baking pan to set.

Repeat the process for the remaining half of the cracker sandwiches, using white chocolate chips this time instead. Allow chocolate to set on a parchment-lined cookie sheet and transfer all the sandwiches to an airtight container.

YIELD: 15 servings

100-Calorie Homemade Snacks

One of the most frequent requests from moms in my MOMables community is a list of real foods in the 100-calorie range. Here is a short list of some single-serving real food combinations for around 100 calories. Ditch the packaged kind.

- 1 cup (150 g) mixed berries + 2 tablespoons (30 g) yogurt
- 1 Apple Sandwich (page 31)
- 1 cup (255 g) Strawberry Applesauce (page 32)
- 1 Red, White, and Blue Parfait (page 34)
- 1 Chocolate Banana Pop (page 44)
- 1 Watermelon Pop (page 47) + an Oatmeal Raisin Cookie Dough Bite (page 64)
- 1 serving Crunchy Berry Salad (page 47)
- 1 medium orange + 1½ tablespoons (20 g) Dreamsicle Fruit Dip (page 70)
- 1 Pear Crumble (page 89)
- 1 Blueberry Crumble (page 89)
- ½ cup (120 g) Chocolate Chia Seed Mousse (page 113)
- ¼ cup (16 g) Cheese Snack Crackers (page 138)
- 2 Deviled Egg Halves (pages 150–151)
- 1 Strawberries and Cream Rice Cake (page 156)
- ½ English Muffin Pizza (page 162)
- 1 serving Super Hero Smoothie (page 187)
- 1 serving Super Green Smoothie (page 187)
- 1 Mango Freeze Pop (page 206)
- 1 Strawberry Yogurt Freeze Pop (page 209)
- 1 Fresh Fruit and Lemonade Pop (page 215)
- ½ cup (120 g) Kiwi Ice Cream (page 215)

Feedback Chart

Use this section as a guide to track all of the delicious snacks you've created from this book. Let the kids fill in the star ratings so it's quick and easy to go back and find their favorites!

RECIPE	DATE MADE	KID STAR RATING (Fill in the stars!)	NOTES AND SUBSTITUTIONS (e.g., Any recipe adjustments or variations made? Was this served with other items? Recipe good for make-ahead?)	MAKE AGAIN?
CHAPTER 2: FRUIT AND VEGGIE SNACKS				
Apple Sandwiches (page 31)		☆☆☆☆☆		○ YES ○ NO
Chocolate Avocado Pudding (page 31)		☆☆☆☆☆		○ YES ○ NO
Baked Apple Pie Parfait (page 32)		☆☆☆☆☆		○ YES ○ NO
Strawberry Applesauce (page 32)		☆☆☆☆☆		○ YES ○ NO
Aloha Cups (page 33)		☆☆☆☆☆		○ YES ○ NO
Tropical Parfait (page 33)		☆☆☆☆☆		○ YES ○ NO
Grape and Granola Yogurt Parfait (page 34)		☆☆☆☆☆		○ YES ○ NO
Red, White, and Blue Parfait (page 34)		☆☆☆☆☆		○ YES ○ NO
White Chocolate Raspberries (page 37)		☆☆☆☆☆		○ YES ○ NO
Chocolate Toffee Berries (page 37)		☆☆☆☆☆		○ YES ○ NO
Heavenly Bowl (page 39)		☆☆☆☆☆		○ YES ○ NO
Easy Strawberry Cheesecake Bites (page 39)		☆☆☆☆☆		○ YES ○ NO
Tropical Fruit Cups (page 40)		☆☆☆☆☆		○ YES ○ NO
Grape Poppers (page 40)		☆☆☆☆☆		○ YES ○ NO

RECIPE	DATE MADE	KID STAR RATING	NOTES AND SUBSTITUTIONS	MAKE AGAIN?
Strawberry Shortcake Kabobs (page 43)		☆☆☆☆☆		○ YES ○ NO
Summer Peach Salad (page 43)		☆☆☆☆☆		○ YES ○ NO
Tropical Banana Bites (page 44)		☆☆☆☆☆		○ YES ○ NO
Chocolate Banana Pops (page 44)		☆☆☆☆☆		○ YES ○ NO
Watermelon Pops (page 47)		☆☆☆☆☆		○ YES ○ NO
Crunchy Berry Salad (page 47)		☆☆☆☆☆		○ YES ○ NO
Crunchy Apple Cheesecake (page 48)		☆☆☆☆☆		○ YES ○ NO
Mixed Berry and Banana Fruit Salad (page 48)		☆☆☆☆☆		○ YES ○ NO
Ham and Cheese Apple Wraps (page 49)		☆☆☆☆☆		○ YES ○ NO
Oven-Fried Bananas (page 49)		☆☆☆☆☆		○ YES ○ NO
Veggie Dipping Jars (page 51)		☆☆☆☆☆		○ YES ○ NO
Italian Flag Bites (page 51)		☆☆☆☆☆		○ YES ○ NO
Mediterranean Cucumber (page 52)		☆☆☆☆☆		○ YES ○ NO
Chocolate Covered Kiwi Pops Cups (page 52)		☆☆☆☆☆		○ YES ○ NO
Tuna Salad Cucumber Cups (page 54)		☆☆☆☆☆		○ YES ○ NO
Caprese Skewers (page 54)		☆☆☆☆☆		○ YES ○ NO
Easy Strawberry Jam (page 56)		☆☆☆☆☆		○ YES ○ NO
CHAPTER 3: NO-BAKE BITES AND DIPS				
Blueberry Vanilla Granola Bars (page 59)		☆☆☆☆☆		○ YES ○ NO
Winnie-the-Pooh Snacks (page 60)		☆☆☆☆☆		○ YES ○ NO

RECIPE	DATE MADE	KID STAR RATING	NOTES AND SUBSTITUTIONS	MAKE AGAIN?
Brown Rice Krispy Treats (page 60)		☆☆☆☆☆		○ YES ○ NO
Drop Cookies (page 63)		☆☆☆☆☆		○ YES ○ NO
Chocolate Peanut Butter Pretzel Haystacks (page 63)		☆☆☆☆☆		○ YES ○ NO
Oatmeal Raisin Cookie Dough Bites (page 64)		☆☆☆☆☆		○ YES ○ NO
Chocolate Brownie Energy Bites (page 64)		☆☆☆☆☆		○ YES ○ NO
Chocolate Banana Mini Pretzelwiches (page 67)		☆☆☆☆☆		○ YES ○ NO
Bananas Gone Nuts! (page 67)		☆☆☆☆☆		○ YES ○ NO
Monkey Kisses (page 68)		☆☆☆☆☆		○ YES ○ NO
Birthday Cake Bites (page 68)		☆☆☆☆☆		○ YES ○ NO
Chocolate Strawberry Shortcakes (page 69)		☆☆☆☆☆		○ YES ○ NO
Caramel Cheesecake Apple Dip (page 69)		☆☆☆☆☆		○ YES ○ NO
Lemonade Stand Fruit Dip (page 70)		☆☆☆☆☆		○ YES ○ NO
Dreamsicle Fruit Dip (page 70)		☆☆☆☆☆		○ YES ○ NO
Maple Cinnamon Dip (page 70)		☆☆☆☆☆		○ YES ○ NO
Blueberry Lemon-Flavored Cream Cheese (page 72)		☆☆☆☆☆		○ YES ○ NO
Cinnamon Roll-Flavored Cream Cheese (page 72)		☆☆☆☆☆		○ YES ○ NO
Peaches and Cream Flavored Cream Cheese (page 73)		☆☆☆☆☆		○ YES ○ NO
Savory Herb-Flavored Cream Cheese (page 73)		☆☆☆☆☆		○ YES ○ NO
Homemade Hummus (page 74)		☆☆☆☆☆		○ YES ○ NO
Edamame Hummus (page 74)		☆☆☆☆☆		○ YES ○ NO

RECIPE	DATE MADE	KID STAR RATING	NOTES AND SUBSTITUTIONS	MAKE AGAIN?
Fresh Herb Yogurt Dip (page 76)		☆☆☆☆☆		○ YES ○ NO
Homemade Pesto (page 76)		☆☆☆☆☆		○ YES ○ NO
Eggplant Dip (page 77)		☆☆☆☆☆		○ YES ○ NO
Blue Cheese Yogurt Dip (page 77)		☆☆☆☆☆		○ YES ○ NO
Yanni's Greek Dip (page 77)		☆☆☆☆☆		○ YES ○ NO
Peach Salsa (page 79)		☆☆☆☆☆		○ YES ○ NO
Baked Hummus and Spinach Dip (page 79)		☆☆☆☆☆		○ YES ○ NO
CHAPTER 4: BAKED BITES				
Coffee Shop Blueberry Cake (page 81)		☆☆☆☆☆		○ YES ○ NO
Carrot Cake Overnight Scones (page 83)		☆☆☆☆☆		○ YES ○ NO
Basic Granola Bars (page 84)		☆☆☆☆☆		○ YES ○ NO
Magic Banana Cookies (page 85)		☆☆☆☆☆		○ YES ○ NO
Blueberry Snack Cookies (page 85)		☆☆☆☆☆		○ YES ○ NO
Peaches and Cream Bread (page 86)		☆☆☆☆☆		○ YES ○ NO
Pear Crumble (page 89)		☆☆☆☆☆		○ YES ○ NO
Blueberry Crumble (page 89)		☆☆☆☆☆		○ YES ○ NO
Carrot Cake Muffins (page 90)		☆☆☆☆☆		○ YES ○ NO
Carrot and Zucchini Bars (page 91)		☆☆☆☆☆		○ YES ○ NO
Oatmeal Banana Muffins (page 91)		☆☆☆☆☆		○ YES ○ NO
Cherry Hand Pies (page 92)		☆☆☆☆☆		○ YES ○ NO

RECIPE	DATE MADE	KID STAR RATING	NOTES AND SUBSTITUTIONS	MAKE AGAIN?
Peach Squares (page 94)		☆☆☆☆☆		○ YES ○ NO
Soft Fig Cookies (page 95)		☆☆☆☆☆		○ YES ○ NO
Coconut Macaroons (page 97)		☆☆☆☆☆		○ YES ○ NO
Energy Squares (page 97)		☆☆☆☆☆		○ YES ○ NO
Southern Biscuits (page 98)		☆☆☆☆☆		○ YES ○ NO
Strawberry Shortcakes (page 98)		☆☆☆☆☆		○ YES ○ NO
Cinnamon Soft Pretzel Bites (page 101)		☆☆☆☆☆		○ YES ○ NO
Cinnamon Cheese Twists (page 102)		☆☆☆☆☆		○ YES ○ NO
Baked Cheese Twists (page 102)		☆☆☆☆☆		○ YES ○ NO
CHAPTER 5: REIMAGINED CLASSICS				
Auntie's Perfect Pie Dough (page 105)		☆☆☆☆☆		○ YES ○ NO
Chocolate-Covered Peanut Butter Cookies (page 105)		☆☆☆☆☆		○ YES ○ NO
Fresh Fruit Toaster Pastries (page 107)		☆☆☆☆☆		○ YES ○ NO
Homemade S'mores Toaster Pastries (page 108)		☆☆☆☆☆		○ YES ○ NO
Homemade Minty Thins (page 111)		☆☆☆☆☆		○ YES ○ NO
White Chocolate Raspberry Thins (page 111)		☆☆☆☆☆		○ YES ○ NO
Chocolate Chia Seed Mousse (page 113)		☆☆☆☆☆		○ YES ○ NO
Leftover-Rice Pudding (page 113)		☆☆☆☆☆		○ YES ○ NO
Three-Ingredient Peanut Butter Pudding (page 113)		☆☆☆☆☆		○ YES ○ NO
Gelatin Jigglers (page 114)		☆☆☆☆☆		○ YES ○ NO

RECIPE	DATE MADE	KID STAR RATING	NOTES AND SUBSTITUTIONS	MAKE AGAIN?
Fruit Gummy Snacks (page 114)		☆☆☆☆☆		◯ YES ◯ NO
Apples and Cinnamon Fruit Leather (page 117)		☆☆☆☆☆		◯ YES ◯ NO
Mango Fruit Leather (page 118)		☆☆☆☆☆		◯ YES ◯ NO
Marshmallow Cream Fluff (page 118)		☆☆☆☆☆		◯ YES ◯ NO
Marshmallow Cream–Filled Chocolate Cupcakes (page 119)		☆☆☆☆☆		◯ YES ◯ NO
Homemade Tortilla Chips (page 121)		☆☆☆☆☆		◯ YES ◯ NO
Cinnamon and Sugar Baked Sweet Potato Chips (page 121)		☆☆☆☆☆		◯ YES ◯ NO
Savory Baked Sweet Potato (page 122)		☆☆☆☆☆		◯ YES ◯ NO
Baked Potato Chips Chips (page 122)		☆☆☆☆☆		◯ YES ◯ NO
Homemade Banana Chips (page 124)		☆☆☆☆☆		◯ YES ◯ NO
Zucchini Chips (page 124)		☆☆☆☆☆		◯ YES ◯ NO
Baked Cinnamon Tortilla Chips (page 125)		☆☆☆☆☆		◯ YES ◯ NO
Baked Apple Chips (page 125)		☆☆☆☆☆		◯ YES ◯ NO
Granola Trail Mix (page 127)		☆☆☆☆☆		◯ YES ◯ NO
Caramel Apple Trail Mix (page 127)		☆☆☆☆☆		◯ YES ◯ NO
Homemade Microwave Popcorn (page 128)		☆☆☆☆☆		◯ YES ◯ NO
Southern California Trail Mix (page 128)		☆☆☆☆☆		◯ YES ◯ NO
Tropical Snowman Trail Mix (page 130)		☆☆☆☆☆		◯ YES ◯ NO
S'mores Trail Mix (page 130)		☆☆☆☆☆		◯ YES ◯ NO
Pantry Granola (page 131)		☆☆☆☆☆		◯ YES ◯ NO

RECIPE	DATE MADE	KID STAR RATING	NOTES AND SUBSTITUTIONS	MAKE AGAIN?
Maple Cinnamon Roasted Chickpeas (page 132)		☆☆☆☆☆		○ YES ○ NO
S'mores Popcorn (page 132)		☆☆☆☆☆		○ YES ○ NO
Homemade Caramel Corn (page 133)		☆☆☆☆☆		○ YES ○ NO
Oh-My-Goodness! Party Mix (page 135)		☆☆☆☆☆		○ YES ○ NO
Homemade Golden Fishies (page 137)		☆☆☆☆☆		○ YES ○ NO
Cheese Snack Crackers (page 138)		☆☆☆☆☆		○ YES ○ NO
Homemade Thin Wheat Crackers (page 141)		☆☆☆☆☆		○ YES ○ NO
Homemade Graham Crackers (page 142)		☆☆☆☆☆		○ YES ○ NO
Refried Bean Dip (page 143)		☆☆☆☆☆		○ YES ○ NO
Momveeta Cheese (page 144)		☆☆☆☆☆		○ YES ○ NO
Game Day Dip (page 144)		☆☆☆☆☆		○ YES ○ NO
Homemade Queso Dip (page 146)		☆☆☆☆☆		○ YES ○ NO
Homemade BBQ Beef Jerky (page 146)		☆☆☆☆☆		○ YES ○ NO
CHAPTER 6: MINI MEALS				
Avocado Egg Salad Wraps (page 149)		☆☆☆☆☆		○ YES ○ NO
Easy-to-Peel Hard Boiled Eggs (page 149)		☆☆☆☆☆		○ YES ○ NO
Classic Deviled Eggs (page 150)		☆☆☆☆☆		○ YES ○ NO
Greek Deviled Eggs (page 150)		☆☆☆☆☆		○ YES ○ NO
Avocado Deviled Eggs (page 151)		☆☆☆☆☆		○ YES ○ NO
Pesto Deviled Eggs (page 151)		☆☆☆☆☆		○ YES ○ NO

RECIPE	DATE MADE	KID STAR RATING	NOTES AND SUBSTITUTIONS	MAKE AGAIN?
Pesto Tortilla Pinwheels (page 152)		☆☆☆☆☆		○ YES ○ NO
Peanut Butter Apple Wraps (page 155)		☆☆☆☆☆		○ YES ○ NO
Elvis Rice Cakes (page 155)		☆☆☆☆☆		○ YES ○ NO
Strawberries and Cream Rice Cakes (page 156)		☆☆☆☆☆		○ YES ○ NO
Lox Rice Cakes (page 156)		☆☆☆☆☆		○ YES ○ NO
Peanut Butter Cup Rice Cakes (page 157)		☆☆☆☆☆		○ YES ○ NO
Cinnamon-Raisin Rice Cakes (page 157)		☆☆☆☆☆		○ YES ○ NO
Mini Cuban Sandwiches (page 158)		☆☆☆☆☆		○ YES ○ NO
Kid Crunchy Rolls (page 158)		☆☆☆☆☆		○ YES ○ NO
Pizza Poppers (page 159)		☆☆☆☆☆		○ YES ○ NO
Honey Wheat Biscuits (page 160)		☆☆☆☆☆		○ YES ○ NO
Favorite Friday Night Pizza (page 161)		☆☆☆☆☆		○ YES ○ NO
Biscuit Pizzas (page 162)		☆☆☆☆☆		○ YES ○ NO
English Muffin Pizzas (page 162)		☆☆☆☆☆		○ YES ○ NO
Berry Chocolatey Pizza (page 165)		☆☆☆☆☆		○ YES ○ NO
Savory Tomato Biscuitwiches (page 165)		☆☆☆☆☆		○ YES ○ NO
Bacon-Wrapped Potatoes (page 166)		☆☆☆☆☆		○ YES ○ NO
Fluffy Pigs (page 166)		☆☆☆☆☆		○ YES ○ NO
Pizza Breadsticks (page 168)		☆☆☆☆☆		○ YES ○ NO
Pizza Bagels (page 169)		☆☆☆☆☆		○ YES ○ NO

RECIPE	DATE MADE	KID STAR RATING	NOTES AND SUBSTITUTIONS	MAKE AGAIN?
Mini Fruit Bagel Pizzas (page 169)		☆☆☆☆☆		○ YES ○ NO
Basic Crêpes (page 171)		☆☆☆☆☆		○ YES ○ NO
Awesome Banana Crêpes (page 171)		☆☆☆☆☆		○ YES ○ NO
Mediterranean Crêpes (page 172)		☆☆☆☆☆		○ YES ○ NO
Apple and Cheddar Crêpes (page 172)		☆☆☆☆☆		○ YES ○ NO
Broccoli and Cheese Crêpes (page 173)		☆☆☆☆☆		○ YES ○ NO
Blueberry Quesadilla (page 173)		☆☆☆☆☆		○ YES ○ NO
Spinach and Artichoke Cups (page 174)		☆☆☆☆☆		○ YES ○ NO
DIY Nachos (page 174)		☆☆☆☆☆		○ YES ○ NO
Tex-Mex Chicken Salad Bites (page 177)		☆☆☆☆☆		○ YES ○ NO
Southwest Chicken Salad (page 177)		☆☆☆☆☆		○ YES ○ NO
Ninja Turtle Nuggets (page 178)		☆☆☆☆☆		○ YES ○ NO
Baked Zucchini Bites (page 178)		☆☆☆☆☆		○ YES ○ NO
CHAPTER 7: SUPER SMOOTHIES AND DRINKS				
Elvis Shakes (page 183)		☆☆☆☆☆		○ YES ○ NO
Banana Blueberry Orange Smoothie (page 183)		☆☆☆☆☆		○ YES ○ NO
Berry Banana Smoothie (page 183)		☆☆☆☆☆		○ YES ○ NO
Mango Peach Smoothie (page 184)		☆☆☆☆☆		○ YES ○ NO
Summer Blush Smoothie (page 184)		☆☆☆☆☆		○ YES ○ NO
Raisin Paste (page 185)		☆☆☆☆☆		○ YES ○ NO
Super Hero Smoothie (page 187)		☆☆☆☆☆		○ YES ○ NO

RECIPE	DATE MADE	KID STAR RATING	NOTES AND SUBSTITUTIONS	MAKE AGAIN?
Super Green Smoothie (page 187)		☆☆☆☆☆		○ YES ○ NO
Tropical Smoothie (page 188)		☆☆☆☆☆		○ YES ○ NO
Apple Quinoa Smoothie (page 188)		☆☆☆☆☆		○ YES ○ NO
Antioxidant Smoothie (page 189)		☆☆☆☆☆		○ YES ○ NO
Thick and Creamy Dairy-Free Yogurt (page 190)		☆☆☆☆☆		○ YES ○ NO
Homemade Yogurt Drink (page 190)		☆☆☆☆☆		○ YES ○ NO
Homemade Hot Chocolate (page 193)		☆☆☆☆☆		○ YES ○ NO
Homemade Sports Drink (page 193)		☆☆☆☆☆		○ YES ○ NO
DIY Hot Cocoa Mix (page 194)		☆☆☆☆☆		○ YES ○ NO
Real Fruit Punch (page 194)		☆☆☆☆☆		○ YES ○ NO
Homemade Icy Drink (page 194)		☆☆☆☆☆		○ YES ○ NO
OJ Cubes (page 197)		☆☆☆☆☆		○ YES ○ NO
Raspberry Green Tea (page 197)		☆☆☆☆☆		○ YES ○ NO
Fruit Ice Cubes (page 197)		☆☆☆☆☆		○ YES ○ NO
Homemade Lemonade (page 199)		☆☆☆☆☆		○ YES ○ NO
Lemonade Granita (page 199)		☆☆☆☆☆		○ YES ○ NO
Blackberry Ginger Lemonade (page 200)		☆☆☆☆☆		○ YES ○ NO
Strawberry Lemonade (page 200)		☆☆☆☆☆		○ YES ○ NO

CHAPTER 8: FROZEN DELIGHTS AND SPECIAL TREATS

RECIPE	DATE MADE	KID STAR RATING	NOTES AND SUBSTITUTIONS	MAKE AGAIN?
Chocolate Hazelnut Banana Ice Cream (page 205)		☆☆☆☆☆		○ YES ○ NO
Homemade Chocolate Hazelnut Spread (page 205)		☆☆☆☆☆		○ YES ○ NO

RECIPE	DATE MADE	KID STAR RATING	NOTES AND SUBSTITUTIONS	MAKE AGAIN?
Cinnamon Dulce Banana Ice Cream (page 205)		☆☆☆☆☆		○ YES ○ NO
Aloha Ice Cream Pops (page 206)		☆☆☆☆☆		○ YES ○ NO
Mango Freeze Pops (page 206)		☆☆☆☆☆		○ YES ○ NO
Strawberry Yogurt Freeze Pops (page 209)		☆☆☆☆☆		○ YES ○ NO
Frozen Yogurt Blueberry Bites (page 209)		☆☆☆☆☆		○ YES ○ NO
Easy Strawberries and Cream Ice Cream (page 210)		☆☆☆☆☆		○ YES ○ NO
Peanut Butter and Honey Banana Ice Cream (page 210)		☆☆☆☆☆		○ YES ○ NO
Monkey Ice Cream Sandwiches (page 211)		☆☆☆☆☆		○ YES ○ NO
Strawberry Cheesecake Ice Cream Sandwiches (page 211)		☆☆☆☆☆		○ YES ○ NO
Pineapple Whip Ice Cream (page 212)		☆☆☆☆☆		○ YES ○ NO
Banana Split Freeze Pops (page 212)		☆☆☆☆☆		○ YES ○ NO
Chocolate Super Pops (page 213)		☆☆☆☆☆		○ YES ○ NO
Green Super Pops (page 213)		☆☆☆☆☆		○ YES ○ NO
Fresh Fruit and Lemonade Pops (page 215)		☆☆☆☆☆		○ YES ○ NO
Kiwi Ice Cream (page 215)		☆☆☆☆☆		○ YES ○ NO
Homemade Almond Butter Cups (page 216)		☆☆☆☆☆		○ YES ○ NO
Trail Mix Bites (page 216)		☆☆☆☆☆		○ YES ○ NO
Coconut Almond Bites (page 218)		☆☆☆☆☆		○ YES ○ NO
Frosty Treats (page 218)		☆☆☆☆☆		○ YES ○ NO
Chocolate Covered PB&J Bites (page 219)		☆☆☆☆☆		○ YES ○ NO

Acknowledgments

To Eric, my best friend and love of my life. For being supportive of my dreams regardless how big they might be. Thank you for encouraging me to do what I love and for loving me as I am.

To my kids, Sofia, Alex, and Gabriel. Thank you for sharing your love of snacking with me. You are my inspiration, my gift, and my life's work.

To my parents, John and Isabel. Thank you for sharing with others how proud you are of my accomplishments. It's one thing to know it, and it's another to hear it.

My in-laws, Moose and Debbie. Thank you for another spring and summer of never-ending support and help with the kids. I couldn't do it without you.

To my family and friends. Thank you for being a part of my life. Your support over the past few years of a company launch, development of cookbooks, constant travel, and crazy ideas mean the world to me.

My MOMables team: You are truly amazing. Thank you for knowing when to step in to help with test recipes and work on cookbooks when I'm busy traveling and being mom ... and when I disappear off the radar for a week or so.

My friend, Alison Bickel: Because together, we make a better team. You are able to capture with a camera how I see food in my mind so I can share it with others.

To the thousands of parents in the MOMables community. You inspire me and make me want to work harder to find ways to help you make real food convenient and appealing to kids.

To Amanda, my editor, and the Fair Winds publishing team. Thank you for trusting that I could deliver a second cookbook. Thank you for listening, answering my many emails, and having my back in the publishing world.

To our Creator. With you, all things are possible.

About the Author

Laura Fuentes is the founder and CEO of MOMables.com, where she helps thousands of parents every day make lunches their kids will love. She is also the author of *The Best Homemade Kids' Lunches on the Planet* (Fair Winds Press, 2014) and a contributor to numerous magazines and online publications.

A speaker, recipe developer, and lover of all things mom, Laura does everything she can to promote healthy school lunches, inspire parents to make more homemade meals, and encourage healthy family eating.

In her personal blog, Laura writes about motherhood, good family food, managing deadlines, and keeping her cool (even when her kids super-glued her hair). To find out more about Laura, visit www.LauraFuentes.com.

Index